GEORGE HANDEL HILL.

Yours Truly
G. H. Hill

LIFE AND RECOLLECTIONS

OF

YANKEE HILL:

TOGETHER WITH

ANECDOTES AND INCIDENTS

OF

HIS TRAVELS.

EDITED BY

DR. W. K. NORTHALL.

NEW-YORK,
PUBLISHED FOR MRS. CORDELIA HILL,
BY W. F. BURGESS, 22 ANN STREET.
1850.

INTRODUCTION.

It is to be regretted some means cannot be discovered whereby the impression which the player makes by his acting could be Daguerreotyed, so that his pictures may be handed down to posterity, that those who follow after us may know what manner of man he was. The immortality which crowns the labors of the painter in a great measure depends upon the durability of the material he employs in his art. If the splendid conceptions of Raphael had faded from the canvass upon which they were realized, as speedily as those of the Actor fade from the public memory when he is no longer able to make them palpable, the Player's art would not suffer, as it does now, from comparison with that of the Painter. It requires as high a degree of intellect to embody a living representation of character on the stage as it does to impress it on canvass, and the Painter has only the advantage of being able to render that lasting which is evanescent and short-lived with the Player.

No matter what command of language the Biographer of an eminent Actor may possess, what skill he may employ in the detail and management of his subject, it is utterly impossible for him, in language, to convey a full and nice appreciation of those fine qualities of his genius which spoke from the eye, were felt in the tones of the voice, and gave meaning to the very slightest action of the body. In writing the Biography of Mr. Hill, whose fame as a delineator of a peculiar class of character is co-extensive with the land that gave him birth, I cannot but feel all the difficulties and embarrassments which arise from a want of means, as well as power to do justice to his character as an actor, and if it were not that I am addressing thousands who have seen him, and whose memories will supply that which language cannot convey, I should feel almost disposed to abandon the task I have assumed, in despair. It is a common error with a certain class of people, to suppose that a man who devotes his time and life to the amusement of the public, has no higher claims to the respect of the community than those which might be preferred by the dancing monkey. I have yet to learn, however, that the wit which can make the judicious smile, is less a spark of heavenly fire than the pathos which can make the tender weep. If people are easier made to laugh than cry, it is rather a strong motive for believing that God designed that mirth should be the rule and weeping the exception; and he, in my opinion, who devotes his life to humanize the over long-drawn solemn face, people a desert of wrinkles with cheerful spirits, and relieve the lachrymal gland from an eternal flow of tears, thus saving a thousand cheerful impulses from a watery grave, lives to accomplish a noble purpose, and should command admiration in his vocation, rather than the obloquy too frequently bestowed upon his efforts. The man who goes about continually moaning and groaning, stereotyping his face into a fixed misery, is a fool to himself and an ingrate to his God. The birds are cheerful at all times, in season, the flowers are decked in the gayest colors, and is man, made in the image of his God, to go sneaking through the world as though he had no business in it, and as though he must make himself miserable in order to be happy? The Actor's art has higher aims and nobler purposes than the Aminadab Sleeks of the day are willing to award it; and the time, I trust, is not far distant when the stage, purified from the adventitious evils which have grown around it, will justify itself, and take its proper place among the highest and surest means of reforming and elevating society. I have spoken thus freely, because I have undertaken the biography of Mr. HILL, "with a will," and I would have those whom I shall address, believe that I would not have undertaken the editing of a mere jest book, for neither humor nor wit have any dignity, in my mind, unless they are employed to effect some good object or illustrate a valued truth. It is the conviction that Mr. Hill accomplished a useful and honorable destiny, which makes me feel desirous to be, in part, the means of preserving as far as possible the memory of the man and his deeds.

BIOGRAPHICAL SKETCH.

George Handel Hill was born in the city of Boston, in the year 1809. His father, Uri K. Hill, enjoyed some reputation in the musical world. The late Samuel Woodworth, the well-known author of the "Moss-covered Bucket," in a brief sketch which he left of the early career of his friend, Mr. Hill, humorously supposes that the reverence in which the father held the memory of the great composer, was the cause of George having a *Handel* to his name.

At an early age, he was placed in the Taunton Academy, it being ultimately intended that he should enter the Harvard University, to become fitted for the practice of whichever of the learned professions his taste might select. Alas! as Burns says, "the best laid schemes are mice, and we oft gang aglee," and ere even all the honors of the Taunton Academy had crowned the labors of our hero, a seed, sown no one knows how, had begun to germinate in his mind, which soon grew up a shrub of vigorous promise.

Young Hill had a keen appreciation of the humorous and ridiculous, and being gifted with unusual powers of imitation, soon made himself notorious among his schoolmates as a fellow "of infinite jest," whom to see in his merry moments, was to them "as good as a play."

The admiration which his juvenile efforts elicted from his school-fellows, made him ambitious to improve his abilities, and perhaps at this time he imbibed the first desire to gain a larger stage for the exhibition of his comic talents. Study, to a boy of his mercurial temperament and humorous disposition, was, as can easily be imagined, at best but dull work. His parents, of course, were grieved that the Taunton Academy had so little fascination for him, or that Harvard University in perspective, could not win from him a more sturdy application to severe study. The *vis comica* was in him, and neither the hopes of collegiate honors, nor the parental frowns, could drive this supposed enemy from the strong hold it had upon his mind.

At the age of 15 he gave up his studies, and, without the consent of those who had a right to control his actions at that age, repaired to New York, to seek his fortune. If boys could only look beyond the romance which youthful imagination raises between their present and their future, and see the struggles and difficulties which beset unaided merit, no matter how great, I fancy there are few of them would turn a deaf ear to parental warning, or leave a cheerful fire-side for the certain miseries of a too early entrance upon the stage of life. Parents, on the other hand, should be very careful how they render the homes of their children unattractive, by a too severe bending of natural impulses to supposed duties. No impulse which leads a child to an honest pursuit, however different from the one selected or desired, should be inconsiderately checked, particularly where the impulse is accompanied with unmistakeable evidence of genius. Many a youth, who has abandoned his home for the pursuits of a theatrical career, and has afterwards been left a floating atom on the sea of life, driven to and fro, without guide or compass, by every fitful wind that blew, would, under a more kindly guidance, have become, not only a brilliant ornament in the profession of his adoption, but what is better, would have been as respectable in moral conduct, as admirable in dramatic ability. Luckily for our young adventurer, his love of the Drama was subordinate to the lessons of morality he had been taught at home, and whilst his heart was in the Theatre, he never forgot his accountability to society for his bearing and conduct. On his arrival at New York he sought employment, and found it at a jeweler's store in Chatham street, where he was engaged as a clerk. He was, at this time, but 15 years of age.

In selecting a place in Chatham street, he had, doubtless, his eye to a Theatrical neighborhood, for the store in which he was engaged was next door, or near Barrere's Garden, a famous place of amusement in those days. It is not very wonderful that, with the strong predilections which he had for the stage, he should have a congenial admiration for the Players. He soon contrived to form an acquaintance with some of the Actors engaged in the neighboring establishment. This led to an introduction behind the scenes. The gates of his paradise being thus open to his *entrée*, he soon became desirous of being something more than a mere looker on ;—he was anxious to hold a closer communion with the kings, dukes, and princes which nightly assembled. But the aforesaid dignitaries, however familiar in their *lucid* intervals, could not allow a sudden and too familiar approach, and young Hill, with all his earnest longing, and vaulting ambition, had to learn, that the way to a throne or principality is beset with thorns and difficulties: but he had "that within that passeth show," and he submitted with a good grace to the necessity of beginning at the beginning, feeling confident that at no remote period, he would rule where he was now serving.

His first appearance on the stage was in a Roman mob, whose duty it was to throw up greasy caps to Coriolanus, and shout when the prompter gave the cue. He was an Actor now, and although he played no very important part in the Drama, there is but little doubt he thought *his* shout was a little the loudest, the strongest, and the most Roman of them all. After a while, he was, as a favor, entrusted to deliver short messages upon the stage. In this rather difficult duty he acquitted himself to the satisfaction of all concerned.

Young Hill now formed an unalterable determination to adopt the stage as his profession. It does not appear that he had determined upon any particular walk of the Drama, or had even asked himself the question what was the line of business for which he was best fitted. The Yankee character, in the delineation of which he afterwards became so famous, had never been presented on the stage with any success, and of course, adopting the Yankee as his starting point never occurred to him. (Mr. Hackett had not yet made his appearance, nor did he, until 1826, one year after Mr. Hill had made the Yankee peculiarly his own.)

In the year 1825, Woodworth's pastoral Opera of the Forest Rose was produced; the part of "Jonathan," the Yankee, was entrusted to Alexander Simpson. Although the character of "Jonathan" is a mere sketch, Mr. Simpson managed to make it a very amusing part to the audience, who nightly thronged to witness the production of a native author. The effect produced upon young Hill was such, as at once determined him to make the Yankee character his study. The success which afterwards crowned his efforts showed how well he had judged his own capabilities. His mind decided upon the particular path he should travel on the road to fame and fortune; he desired nothing so much as an opportunity of appearing in his favorite character. Whilst at the Chatham Street Theatre, engaged in the way we have already noticed, he was introduced to a country manager, who readily engaged him for the low comedian of his company, which was about to make a theatrical tour through the western part of the State of New York. I believe during this engagement he had no opportunity of appearing in his favorite character, the Yankee,—yet the arrangement was full of satisfaction, for he not only acquired confidence and experience, but great popularity; he became a favorite wherever he appeared. Mr. Hill's comedy consisted, as he himself afterwards expressed it, in grimacing,—or, technically, mug-making. During this engagement, he met, at Stafford, with the "Methodical Audience," whose serious character he used to represent so inimitably in his entertainments. The good people of Stafford, it appears, had been unused to theatrical representations,—the company, of which Mr. Hill was then a member, being the first dramatic corps which had ever appeared among them. On the opening night of the Theatre, alias ball-room, the tragedy of William Tell was played, to be succeeded by the farce of the "Lady and the Devil." When the audience assembled, the women were found seated on one side of the room, and the men on the other, exactly as they had been accustomed at church. During the performance of the tragedy, the most solemn stillness was observed: not a hand rewarding the poor Actor for his exertions. No one but the player can tell the dull, hard labor of performing a long, heavy part, unrelieved by the inspiring influence of a round of applause. Even the ceremony of hoisting the star-spangled banner above the pole upon which Gezlar's cap was placed, failed to excite any palpable emotion. The audience were evidently on their best behavior. The curtain went down upon the tragedy like a pall. Mr Hill was cast for the low comedy part in the farce, and although he was somewhat disheartened by the cold character of the audience before which he was about to appear, he determined to exert himself to the utmost to break the ice which seemed to encase each individual present. Mr. Hill made more grimaces on this occasion than he ever employed before or afterwards, and did more illegitimate things than ever actor dreamed of, to make his audience laugh, but it was of no avail, they were immoveable. After the performance, Mr. Hill retired to the public room of the hotel in which he boarded, wearied with his efforts, and mortified with his want of success. He had scarcely seated himself, when he was accosted by a tall, raw-boned countryman.

"Lewk here, mister."

"Well, sir?"

"I've been in to see the play to-night."

"Have you, indeed?" said Mr. Hill, "you must have been highly entertained."

"I swow, I guess I was. I tell you what it is, now; my mouth won't be straight for the next month, straining to keep from larfing. If it hadn't a been far the women, I should a snorted right out in the meetin'."

Mr. Hill was, of course, gratified to find that the solemn behavior of the audience was in obedience to their conventional notions of public conduct, instead of the want of comic merit in his efforts.

Before he had completed his engagement, he met with an accident at Batavia which confined him to his bed for some weeks; and I believe for several months disabled him from performing. He met with the greatest kindness from the hospitable people of that town, which he publicly acknowledged by the following address, delivered at the entertainment he gave on his first appearance in public after the accident:

Address, spoken on Tuesday, March 4th, 1828.

"I bow before you now, not in the comic character which on former occasions has gained your applause and approbation. There are times of sorrow as well as gaiety. The sombre spectres and scenes of death, cannot be always before our eyes, and some light joys must be an antidote to those bitter sorrows we are doomed to suffer. The days of prosperity last not forever; thorns spring upon our pathway that impede our passage. The patronage bestowed upon me in Batavia, and the compliments received shall never be forgotton: this place and these friends shall live in my remembrance whilst the pulsations of the heart beat with all the tenderness of feeling. Honorable exertion in any profession must command the approbation of every honorable mind. By an untoward misfortune I suffer not alone. I have not merely had pains of body and agony of mind proceeding from the calamities which so often embitter our paths on the journey of life, but I am a child, with filial tenderness, bound to protect a mother. In this my native country, where the child of sorrow is never left without pity and sympathy, it has been my pride to appear before you with the tender of my services. Of past kindness I am neither thankless nor neglectful, and the meed of your praise, whilst by your rewards bestowed on my labors, I am enabled to support life, animates me to more vigorous exertions in the discharge of my duties.

"Ladies and Gentlemen, self-praise is no commendation, nor is it a claim which the humble aspirant after fame should arrogate unless it is bestowed. To please and amuse you, I have done and shall do the best in my humble capacity, and with the full flow of a grateful heart offer you my best wishes."

It may be as well to state here that the first entertainment which Mr. Hill gave alone, *à la* Mathews, was in the city of Brooklyn, in the year 1826. The Star, of that period, then under the editorial conduct of Col. Alden Spooner, speaks flatteringly of the young aspirant for dramatic fame, and intimates that at no distant period Mr. Hill will occupy a distinguished place in the Theatrical world.

In the year 1828, Mr. Hill temporarily eschewed "single entertainments," and engaged himself in company for life, with one who faithfully followed his footsteps through all his fortunes to the closing, sad last scene of life. He married Miss Thompson, of Le Roy, an amiable and accomplished young lady, whose parents exacted, as a condition, that he should leave the stage. It is no slight evidence of the strength of his attachment, that he complied with terms which to all appearance were to crush the earnest longings of his heart, and shut out forever from his sight the brilliant future his warm imagination had painted for his own.

He commenced business, but, as may readily be supposed, without success. His heart was not in it. The dull monotony of a store-keeper's life did not suit him ; and after making a short and feeble effort to mercantile his mind, he gave up the struggle and made an engagement with the manager of the Albany Theatre. Mrs. Hill, like a sensible and affectionate woman, did not reproach him with a violation of the condition which her friends made at her marriage, but appreciating the desires and ambition of her husband, and like him, confident in his ability to achieve both fame and fortune, she, as every good wife would do, encouraged and aided him in his efforts. That he felt grateful for the sacrifice which she made for his sake, is evinced by the affectionate character of his communications with her. His letters to her when away, even up to the time when the sickness seized him which ended his career, breathe warm affection in every line. But of this I shall have to speak in another part of his Life. Mr. Hill's success at Albany, was as eminent as his warmest friends could have wished. He was accounted by the critics of that city, one of the most promising young comedians of the day. After leaving Albany, he paid a short visit to Buffalo, and delivered on several occasions, with profit and success, the same entertainment I have stated he gave in Batavia after his accident. He then, with his young wife, returned to New York, and played a short engagement at Peale's Museum. During this visit, he appeared for one evening at Blanchard's Amphitheatre, now the Richmond, and told the following story in his inimitable style:

"Darn my buttons, if I didn't once court a gal by the name of Suky Snow: any on ye hearn tell of Suky? I was detarmined to go and ask her if she'd have me. When I got there, the cat was playin' round the room, and I trod on her tail—I didn't mean tew though—she squalled eout, and Suke jumped up as mad as blazes and threw her out doors. I felt kinder sorry for the cat, 'cause you know any cat will squall if you tread on her tail. I sot down by the winder, and, thinks I—I'll say something now anyhow: says I, Suke, it looks rather green outside reound here: yes says she, and it looks rather green inside tew. Says I, Suke, there's the meetin' house; yes, said she, and there goes the Deacon. Jest as I was goin' to ask her if she would be my lawful wedded wife, her ugly old aunt came to the door, and I run and held it on t'other side; she couldn't git in, and I couldn't git eout; finally I made a bolt for the winder, and out I went into the old woman's soft soap tub; as I was crawling eout, one feller said 'Jest coming down?' No, you tarnal fool, I'm jest comin' up. You needn't larf none on ye—I didn't lose nothin' by it, for I got 'my clothes washed for half price, 'caus they was already soaped.'"

He was next engaged to go South by Mr. Falkener, the Manager of the Charleston Theatre. He played both at Charleston and Savannah, gaining an increasing popularity at every appearance. His star was rapidly rising, and he received the offer of a profitable engagement from Jones, Duffy & Forrest, managers of the Arch Street Theatre of Philadelphia. This engagement forms an important era in the life of Mr. Hill, for it was during the season he played here that he made his first appearance in the Yankee character. His success was such as to place him at once on a level with the best comedians of the day, and far above any as a truthful representative of the genuine down easter. Mr. Hill's Yankee was the "real critter." It was not, as are almost all the representations of other actors I have seen, a mixture of Western, Southern and Eastern peculiarities of manner and dialect, but the unalloyed, unadulterated down-easter. Mr. Hill did not merely imitate their tone, dialect and manner, but felt and thought like them. It was this faculty, to use a hackneyed phrase, of throwing himself, body and spirit, into a part, which gave to his Yankee a richness and truthfulness not approached by any actor before or since his time. He did not merely put on a flaxen wig, a long-tailed coat, a short vest, a bell-crowned hat, and straps to his pantaloons long enough for suspenders, nor thus attired did he content himself by imitating the peculiar drawl and queer expressions of the Yankee, for the veriest bungler on earth can do all this, but the spirit of Yankeedom pervaded every action of his body, peeped from his expressive eyes with such sly meaning, that it was difficult for the time being, not to believe it was a mistake in the bills, when they announced Mr. Hill as Major Wheeler, instead of announcing the veritable Major Wheeler himself. Jonathan, in Woodworth's pastoral opera of the Forest Rose, was the part he selected for his debut in the Yankee character on the occasion referred to.

In the year 1832, he made his first starring engagement at Baltimore with eminent success. In the fall of the same year, he made his debut before a Boston audience. On returning to New York, he was engaged by Mr. Simpson, manager of the Park Theatre. The Park Theatre at that time was to the other cities of the Union, what Covent Garden or Drury Lane Theatres are to the provincial establishments of England, the goal to which all dramatic adventurers aspired. To be engaged on starring terms at the Park, was the actors *ultima thule,* so far as this country was concerned. It is deeply to be regretted, that there is not in New York some establishment bearing the same salutary influence upon the profession, as that which emanated from the Park in its palmy days. There was a power behind the scenes of the Park, which had to be severely satisfied, before the dramatic aspirant could tread the stage; a power above the whims of misdirected public sympathy, and beyond the reach of a merely manufactured popularity; in short, the Park was the head and brains of the American stage. The Yankee character had been introduced as yet in but very few pieces, and Mr. Hill found it necessary to increase his stock of plays. With this view, he offered a prize of four hundred dollars for the best piece adapted to his peculiar style of character. A committee, composed of the following gentlemen—Messrs. Verplanck, Webb, King, and Washington Irving, were chosen to judge of the merits of pieces sent in. Quite a large number of authors competed for the prize, but of all received, the committee did not think one fairly entitled to it. Mr. Hill was, however, much in need of novelty, and at his solicitation alone the prize was awarded to Samuel Woodworth, for a drama, entitled "The Foundling of the Sea." It was produced at the Park on the third engagement of Mr. Hill at that theatre, but was coldly received, and after the third night was withdrawn.

I must now return to Mr. Hill's first engagement with Mr. Simpson. His success was most triumphant, and offers came flowing in from every part of the country. He went next to Philadelphia to play a starring engagement. Mr. Hill's rise in his profession, was deservedly rapid. The public, with a ready appreciation not often awarded, were quick to see the merits of the young comedian, and willing to reward with a generous patronage, the deserts it prided itself in discovering. He now played a brilliant star engagement at Philadelphia, in the same theatre in which, but a few months previously, he had been struggling with an inconsiderable salary of ten dollars a week.

Mr. Hill spent a summer in the Eastern States, for the purpose of studying the Yankee character, and picking up such peculiarities of dialect and expression as he could, from constant communication with the "critters" themselves. In Boston, he was thus invited by a countryman to visit the town in which he lived.

"Wal, Mister Hill, can't you come down our way and give us a show?"

"Where do you live?" inquired Mr. Hill.

"Oh, abeout half way between this ere and sunrise."

"Oh, yes," said Mr. Hill, adopting at once the style of the countryman, "I know;—where the trees grow under ground, and gals weigh two hundred pounds. Where some on 'em are so fat they grease the cart wheels with their shadow, and some on 'em so thin, you are obliged to look at 'em twice afore you can see 'em at all."

"Wal, I guess you've been there:" saying which, the countryman departed.

When a bird flew to pick at a bunch of grapes an artist had painted, it was esteemed the best compliment which could have been paid to the painter. Equally complimentary to the truthfulness of Mr. Hill's Yankee representations, was the flattering mistake related in the following incident:—

Whilst on this visit to the East, Mr. Hill gave an entertainment in Bangor, State of Maine, assisted by the Boston Brass Band. The entertainment was called on the bill "A Musical Olio." In the course of the entertainment, indeed, the first character he represented on this occasion, was that of a country youth. A countryman among the audience would insist upon it that the character on the stage was not Mr. Hill at all, but Seth Snow, a son of one of his neighbors, nor could all the persuasions of those near him convince him of his mistake. As soon as the performance was over, he rushed into Mr. Hill's private room and thus addressed him:—

"Wal, you are doing nice things down here, passing yourself off for Mr. Hill. What d'ye think the old man would say, if he should see you in them play-acting clothes. Oh, you may squirm and twist your tarnal mouth, just abeout as much as you please, but you can't deceive me, so you had better own up. Wal, this is a plaguy nice place; and what a mortal lot of purty picters you've got hanging round. I suppose your getting all fired proud, for you never had such a room tew hum."

Without noticing Mr. Hill further, he turned to look at the pictures which hung around the room. Mr. Hill took advantage of the opportunity, whilst his visitor was thus engaged, to pull off his coat and wig. When the countryman had satisfied his curiosity sufficiently, he turned round to speak to his neighbor's son, Seth Snow, when, to his utter astonishment, a perfect stranger stood before him.

"Why! how—here! where is Seth Snow?"

"I am the only person who has been in this room since you were here," said Mr. Hill.

"Dew tell!"

"Fact, upon my honor."

"And you ain't Seth Snow?"

"No; my name is Hill."

"And you don't know Seth Snow?"

"Never had the honor of his acquaintance."

"Well, I never; if I did, may I be darned. You! if it was you, just now looked and talked jest like Seth Snow, and now you are no more like him than you are like my sister Sue. Wal, I never!"

During this dialogue the countryman was examining Mr. Hill with wondering scrutiny, exclaiming every now and then "Wal, I never."

"Look here, Mr. Hill, I hearn the hull of your talk inside there, but I don't think much of that, cause I hears that stuff every day, to hum,—and I've hearn the blowers, (meaning the musicians,) but one part of the show you ain't put out. No gouging, you know! I paid my money and I want to see the hull."

"Beg your pardon, sir, but we have given the whole entertainment."

"No, you ain't: do you see any thing green, eh?"

"I can't im·gine to what you allude. I'm not aware of any omission."

"Oh, come now, don't the bill say that you've got a Olio? now I want to see the critter; I never heard of the animal afore, and I'm death on critters. I thought maybe you did not like to show the critter to the women, but I want to see the Olio."

Mr. Hill, as may be imagined, laughed heartily at the mistake of the countryman, who, when he was made to understand the nature of the Olio, joined in the merriment, shook hands at parting with Mr. Hill, and begged him, if he ever came down his way, not to say anything about the Olio.

When we consider the years of toil and struggle which marked the slow progress of such a man as Edmund Kean—how reluctant the public were to acknowledge this transcendent genius—we cannot but be struck with the good fortune which waited on Mr. Hill in his early career.

One thing, however, must be considered. Mr. Hill was the first to leave his footsteps upon an untrodden path, and, consequently, they could not be conpared to, or confounded with, the tracts of other men. Mr. Kean was travelling on a highway, over which thousands had passed, and were still crowding on. He had, by his energy and genius, to clear the track, before the public eye could rest singly on him, mark the loftiness of his gait, the gracefulness of his carriage, and the intellectual dignity of his whole bearing. Mr. Hill was fortunate in being able to strike out a new path to himself, and equally fortunate in possessing the genius and talent to maintain its undivided possession.

In Cincinnati and Louisville, Mr. Hill played short engagements with credit to himself, and profit to the managements. His company was much sought after, for his amiable and gentlemanly manners, by the first class of citizens, who retained their friendly and respectful regard for him, to the close of his career. His social feeling, his extraordinary faculty of amusing, and his rich and varied store of anecdote and incident, would have rendered any man a desirable companion; but he had, beside all these, a sterling integrity of character, which made him as much valued as a friend, as prized as a social companion.

His engagement at Louisville was a brilliant one: he played to overflowing houses every night. He was next engaged at New Orleans. He left Louisville on board a steamboat commanded by Captain Gay. One evening when the steamboat had been detained an unusual time in taking in wood, and the passengers assembled at the supper-table, a very uncouth fellow was seen seated among the ladies and gentlemen at the Captain's table. The Captain was too busily engaged with his duties to notice the queer guest, who had already attracted the observation of everybody else. His attention was purposely called to the intruder by a gentleman, who seemed to know more of the stranger than he dared to reveal. The uncouth appearance of the stranger, and a steamboat captain's stereotyped regard for his lady passengers, excited the indignation of the commander, and he told the waiter to order the intruder from the table.

"Stranger," says the waiter, "you must vamose from here."

"Dew tell," said he, eating most voraciously all the time.

"Stranger!" exclaimed the waiter.

"Wal, dew let a feller eat his supper," and another leg of broiled chicken was dispatched.

"You must leave the table."

"Why, how you talk!" and again was he at work upon the eatables.

"Captain," said the waiter, "the stranger won't stir."

"He won't stir, eh?" said the Captain, in a rage. "I'll soon see whether I am to be insulted at my own table;"

and with that the irrate Captain sprang from his seat, and seizing the uninvited guest by the collar of his coat, dragged him from the table. The greatest uproar prevailed among the passengers: some were for aiding the Captain, whilst others, seeing no cause of offence, except the mere fact of a stranger—whom, they supposed, had got on board at the last wooding—obtruding his presence in the wrong place, entreated that he might be permitted to remain. To the latter suggestion the Captain was deaf. There could not be two masters to the same boat, and the Captain, considering he had a prior claim, was proceeding, by a sort of *a posteriori* argument, to assert his rights: when the stranger, not relishing the idea of being kicked out, took off his wig, and displayed to the astonished Captain and his passengers, the familiar countenance of a friend and fellow-traveller, Yankee Hill. The mirth that followed was a sufficient reward to Mr. Hill for the risks he ran. Captain Gay was not a little mortified at being so complètely "taken in and done for" by a man whose face was almost as familiar to him as his own. It was suggested by some of the passengers who had begged that the stranger might be left alone, that the Captain should be court-martialed, for attempting to push out of the cabin one of his most respectable passengers.

The idea was very suggestive of fun, and all agreed that a court-martial was a very respectable and useful institution. I do not think it was exactly in order to appoint one of the interested party to preside as judge upon this occasion, but, be that as it may, Mr. Hill was immediately elected to that office. Captain Gay was tried, found guilty, and condemned to be shot, or, rather, to pay the shot for the amount of oysters, champagne, and other fixings, which strict justice deemed necessary to meet the offence he had committed. And so terminated the suit of Jedediah Homebred *vs.* Captain Gay.

Mr. Hill's success in the Crescent City was as triumphant as it could well be. He made many valuable friends during this visit. Among those who took him by the hand were Col. Wade Hampton, of South Carolina, and the late Col. Fitzsimmons of Augusta, Georgia. These very influential gentlemen entertained a warm and sincere friendship for Mr. Hill, during his whole life.

In the month of April, 1834, he returned to New York, occasionally playing in Philadelphia and Albany. In August he retired to Staten Island, and spent a month there, in preparing the Knight of the Golden Fleece, which was to be brought out at the Park in the September following. While at Staten Island, Mr. Blake, late of the Broadway Theatre, waited upon Mr. Hill, and so far won upon his good nature, as to induce him to purchase a piece, called "Major Jack Downing," for which he paid two hundred and fifty dollars. I have reason to know that in this bargain Mr. Hill's judgment was not appealed to, but that his good nature was, most imploringly; and as Mr. Hill's whole career displays a similar yielding to the necessities of others, it will surprise no one who knows the parties, that he was beaten in the bargain. Major Jack Downing was scarcely worth the value of the paper upon which it was written. I cannot let this opportunity escape without paying a just tribute to Mr. Hill's liberality towards those who wrote for him. Persons unacquainted with the greediness and despicable meanness of mannagers generally, towards authors, will ask, why I should pause to pay a special tribute of respect to Mr. Hill, for his liberality in this particular, when it was so obviously his interest to encourage these efforts in his favor. I answer, by stating that it is so unusual for actors or managers, despite their true interests, to display anything like a remunerative liberality towards those who write for them, that it would be like playing the tragedy of Hamlet, and leaving Hamlet's name out by particular desire, to omit the mention of this uncommon quality in the subject of this biographical sketch.

I know but few managers in the United States who have either the far-seeing wisdom, or the liberality, to induce the dramatic mind of the country to exercise itself for the advancement either of their interests, or the interests of the Stage. Gentlemen of education and refinement, accustomed to the associations of polite life, will scarcely be induced to try dramatic literature, where the pay is not only inconsiderable, but doubtful, and the certainty of arrogant assumption, from nine managers out of ten, beyond question.

The Knight of the Golden Fleece, which was prepared during Mr. Hill's sojourn on Staten Island, was produced at the Park in September, and owing principally to Mr. Hill's admirable acting in the character of Si Saco, was successful. Mr. Hill finished his engagement with eclat. He next played in Philadelphia and Pittsburg, then returned to New York, from which place he sailed with Captain Pennoyer for Charleston. He was received in that city with great enthusiasm. He next played a short term in New Orleans. When he was about leaving this city, standing upon the Levee, waiting for his baggage, he was thus addressed by a long lean down-easter.

"Say, yeou, which of these things slips up fust?"

"What?" said Mr. Hill.

"Which of these things slips up fust?"

"Do you mean which steamboat goes up the river first?"

"Yes. I'll be darned if I don't."

"That one," said Mr. Hill, pointing to the nearest.

"I'm in an awful hurry to git eout of this. It is so thundering hot, and I smell the yeller fever all reound."

This individual had a very intellectual forehead, measuring about an inch and a quarter in height, and punched in at the sides to match. His eyes were set deep in their sockets, and something like a pig's, only the color was not as good. His nose pushed boldly out, as it started from the lower part of his forehead, as though it meant to be something, but when it had reached half its destination, it bent suddenly in like a parrot's beak. His upper lip was long and thin, and was stretched on a sort of rack, which was made by a couple of supernumerary teeth, which stuck out very prominently. His chin, too modest to attempt a rivalry with his projecting lip, receded backwards towards the throat, so that, to look at him in front, you did not perceive that he had any chin at all. His hair was very light and bristly. A snuff-colored coat of domestic manufacture adorned the upper part of his person. It was an ancient affair. The velvet was worn from the collar in several places, but which was carefully patched with red flannel, being the nearest approach to the original color of the collar that could be found in his domestic menagerie of reserved rags. The buttons, which one would naturally look for at the bottom of the waist, had wandered up between his shoulders. The coat was remarkably long, extending from high up on the shoulders to the lower part of the calves of his legs. He was slightly round-shouldered, so that when he stood right up, a small lady might have found shelter in a rain storm in the vacancy left between the coat and the back. His pants, to common observers, would have been called too short, but he denied this, averring that his legs were too long for his trowsers. On his arm hung an old-fashioned camblet cloak, with the lining of green baize hanging about a quarter of a yard below the edge of the camblet. He said this was no fault of the lining, anyhow; "it got wet, and t'other shrunk a leetle, but the lining stuck to it like blazes." The Yankee was exceedingly anxious to secure his passage by the first boat, and he sang out to some person, "Say, yeou, where is the Captain of this consarn. Say, yeou, (to some one else,) I want the Captain. Look here, Nigger, show a feller the Captain. Look here, you black sarpint, don't stick out your lips at me. Wal, I swow, I'll give anybody three cents that will show me the Captain."

The Captain, hearing the noise, stepped forward and told the Yankee if he wished to see the Captain, he was commander of the boat.

"Dew tell? Wal, I swan, you have got a kind of commanding way about you, that's a fact."

"What do you wish?" said the Captain.

"Wal, I want a bathe."

"Very well, jump into the river, there is plenty of water."

"I tell you, I want a bathe."

"Well, don't I tell you to jump in, you can swim across if you like; we shall not start just yet."

"I want a bathe to lie down in. Now do you know what I mean, darn you?"

"Oh, you want a berth?"

"Wal, darn you, didn't I say bathe? I know what I'm about, I guess."

"I will accommodate you as far as I can," said the Captain, "but I have nothing but a mattrass to offer, and that is upon the cabin floor."

"Dew tell."

"It is the only one that is vacant, and the cabin floor is covered with them, so you had better secure it at once."

"Wal, then, I guess I'd better turn right in."

I omitted to mention that he carried a valise in his hand. Some one rather impertinently asked him what he had in it.

"Wal," said he, "I don't know that it's any of your business, but I don't mind telling on you. There is two shirts, one clean, t'other dirty; a pair of pants about as good as new, only a leetle worn here and there, and a pair of pistols. D'ye want I should take 'em out and show you."

When he went down to turn in, he put the valise under his head, wrapped his old cloak around him, and threw himself, as he said, "into the arms of omnibus." The mattrasses on the other side of him, were occupied by some rough Kentucky boatmen. In the middle of the night, these men got up and commenced playing cards. No table being handy, they made use of the back of our Yankee friend for one, and chalked the reckoning of the game upon the camblet cloak, which surrounded the body of the unconscious sleeper. They became interested in the game, and began to lay down their cards with a might of fist, and earnestness of manner, which soon roused up our sleeping friend. He attempted to rise, but was held down by one of the party, who exclaimed, "Lie still, stranger, I've only got three to go, and I hold the Jack."

"Never mind, I'm a most smothered here, but go ahead, darn you, play quick and I'll go you halves." He according lay still, until they had finished their game, but whether the Kentucky gambler divided his gains with his table, was never satisfactorily ascertained.

Mr. Hill returned safely to New-York, and played another successful engagement at the Park. He next went to Philadelphia, and from thence to Buffalo, where he played in the summer of 1836. In the fall of this year he played in Petersburgh, Philadelphia, and New-York, prior to his departure for the South. He was engaged at the magnificent St. Charles, in New-Orleans—Mr. Caldwell being manager and proprietor—and he likewise was engaged by old Sol Smith, for Mobile.

Mr. Hill sailed from New-York on the 3d of January, 1837, in the ship "Mississippi," commanded by Captain Robinson. There were a number of passengers beside Mr. Hill. In two or three days, when the sea-sickness had passed away, he began to exert himself to make the time pass merrily along; and to any one acquainted with his power of entertainment, I need scarcely say, how well he succeeded. The day before the ship arrived at New-Orleans, the passengers gave him a supper on board. After supper the following song was sung by Mr. Hill, the passengers taking up the chorus with a will:

Now, friends, the time is near at hand,
When we disperse this jovial band;
But as the hour approaches near,
Let's still enjoy our Captain's cheer.
Where e'er again we meet, my boys,
We'll tell again our present joys:
The many jokes, the pleasing game,
The ladies, and the Captain's fame.
Chorus: Where e'er again, &c.

When first we left the Eastern shore,
The rough, wide ocean to explore,
Our hearts beat high with hope and fears,
The eyes we left afloat in tears;
How soon the change with us appeared,
When free from sickness all was reared—
Our natural mirth was in a glow,
The juice of grape did freely flow.
How soon, &c.

Fill your glasses to the brim,
This drinking wine is not a sin;
God bless you all, on sea or shore,
I trust the world holds many more.
Now as the sparkling wine we sip,
We won't forget this noble ship:
And when I ask it, don't think ill,
A slight remembrance of this HILL.
Now as, &c.

Whilst in New-Orleans, he purchased some real estate in Mobile, for which he paid five thousand dollars. Some time afterward, an old Spanish claim came up for the property, and he lost every cent of his investment. This is only one of a number of speculations in which ill fortune attended him; indeed, I cannot learn that he ever succeeded in realizing anything from any single venture which he made outside of his profession. Mr. Hill was unquestionably the best Yankee on the stage, and the very worst one off. The down-east shrewdness which made his assumption on the stage so rich and racy, formed no part of his character in matters of purchase or barter. He was simplicity itself on such occasions; and when told by friends, of risks he was running, he would answer, "Oh!

my business will come out right, I guess." But he seldom guessed right. His disposition was sanguine and confiding, and he easily fell a prey to designing men. In connection with the purchase of his Mobile property, I may as well relate the following anecdote, inasmuch as it displays the only bit of shrewdness in money matters ever exhibited by him: It appears he consulted Robert Morris, Esq., ex-Post-Master of New-York, on a point of Law—the fee for which advice was five dollars. Mr. Hill visited Mr. Morris, and when the advice was given, he took out his five dollars and laid it before his lawyer. Whether Mr. Morris was astonished to see a player with so large an amount of ready cash or not, I don't pretend to say, but at any rate, he remarked to Mr. Hill, that players were usually very imprudent in money matters, and that he never saw one who knew how to take care of his money.

"Is that your rale opinion of actors?" said Mr. Hill.

"It is;" replied the ex-Postmaster.

"Allow me, then," said Mr. Hill, picking up his money and putting it into his pocket, "to make you acquainted with one who does know how to take care of his money. Good morning, sir." Mr. Morris was too well entertained with the illustration to detain his client, and laughingly, bade him farewell.

After playing his engagement at New-Orleans and Mobile, he returned to New-York. The following lines, addressed to Yankee Hill, he found in one of the daily papers on his arrival in the city:

OUR OWN YANKEE HILL.

New-England, I love thee, dear land of my birth!
The sky-kissing mountains, where liberty roves;
The blossom-gemmed meadows, the sweetest on earth,
Thy bright, sunny fields, and thy musical groves;
Thy landscapes are smiling when summer prevails,
And vocal with melody's amorous trills;
How sweet are thy laughing and musical dales,
How pleasant thy laughing and musical *Hills.*

I've stray'd in the South, o'er savannah and plain,
By flat fields of indigo, cotton and rice,
Through richest plantations of saccharine cane,
And orange-groves breathing of Araby's spice:
But, home of my childhood, while absent from thee,
And feeling I loved thee more fervently still,
How sweet to the wanderer, was it to see,
A laughing and musical New-England *Hill?*

The fair of the South have acknowledged its worth;
So simple, so quiet, so honestly shrewd,
So freight with the richest incentives to mirth,
So richly with wits' sparkling treasures endued.
When Disherwill, Jonathan, Solomon Swop,
With his Green-Mountain Boy, blue devils to kill,
E'en Beauty must laugh till she's ready to drop,
To view in Mobile such a green Yankee Hill.

Then welcome him back, for this Hill is your own,
And a fresh crop of evergreen shadows his brow;
By you were the seeds of his laurels first sown—
Let fashion and opulence foster them now.
The bright smile of Beauty will welcome him home,
The patrons of Genius will honor him still;
The votaries of Comus forbid him to roam,—
All warmly will welcome our own Yankee Hill.

In the spring of 1836 Mr. Hill again appeared at the Park. In the June following he performed two weeks at the Tremont Theatre, Boston. Returning to New York, he played a farewell engagement at the Park previous to his departure for Europe. A few days before he sailed for England he received the following communication :

"NEW YORK, August 2d, 1836.

" *To George H. Hill, Esq., Comedian.*

"DEAR SIR :—At a meeting held this evening, after organization, it was resolved, that the present being a meeting of the personal friends and professional admirers of Mr. George Hill, on learning that it is his intention to visit Europe in the course of the present month, we will invite him to accept a dinner, to be given by us at the City Hotel, on the 8th inst., as a token of our esteem for his personal character and admiration of his professional excellence.

"In accordance with which resolution, we, in the name of the meeting, invite you to a dinner, to be given as an evidence of their and our regard for your private virtues and professional talents, at the time and place above stated.

"B. BATES, *Chairman.*

"B. BIGNALL,
"S. JENKS SMITH, } *Secretaries.*"

The dinner was given at the City Hotel, at that time *the* Hotel of New York. It was numerously attended. The following letters were read after the cloth was removed:

"PROVIDENCE, August 6th, 1836.

"DEAR SIR :—It is with unfeigned regret that I inform you of my inability to be present at the dinner to be given to our friend Mr. Hill, prior to his departure for Europe. A letter from you first introduced Mr. Hill to my acquaintance, and I ought, long ere this time, to have acknowledged my indebtedness to you for the pleasure I have derived from that acquaintance. He is too well known in his career before the public, to allow me to say, that, as a friend, a true-hearted one, and as a gentleman, I esteem him most highly. May he be a star in Europe, and succeed in showing John Bull what brother Jonathan is in his true character. I will thank you to show him this letter, and present him my warmest regards. I forward you a sentiment for this occasion:

"*The Yankee Character.* It has been perverted and maligned by the Halls and Trollopes of Europe. If through the modesty of our countrymen its beauty has been 'hid under a bushel,' may it soon be seen 'on the house-top,' and conspicuous on the *Hill.*"

"Yours, with respect,

"W. R. Danforth.

"S. J. Smith, Esq."

"New York, August 8th, 1836.

"Sir:—Your note of the 5th inst. did not come to hand in time for an earlier reply. I regret that it is not in my power to avail myself of the very kind invitation of the Committee to be present at the dinner to be given to Mr. Hill, being on the point of setting off for the country. I beg you to make my grateful acknowledgments to the Committee for the honor they have done me, and believe me, very respectfully, your obliged obd't servant,

"Washington Irving."

"S. Jenks Smith, Esq."

On this pleasant occasion he was presented with a silver pitcher, which bore the following inscription:

PRESENTED TO
GEORGE H. HILL, ESQ.,
AS A SLIGHT TOKEN OF THE RESPECT AND ESTEEM
OF A FEW OF HIS
YANKEE FRIENDS IN NEW YORK.

The compliment of such a presentation had at that time an intrinsic value. It had not then, as now, become an idle ceremony, indiscriminately bestowed upon the undeserving and the deserving. A captain of a vessel, now-a-days, who is simply civil to his passengers and is careful and prudent in the conduct of his ship, where his own life and interests are at stake, is so often made the recipient of a compliment of this kind, that the thing has degenerated into a senseless farce. Mr. Hill used to tell a story of a presentation scene he once witnessed in a country town in the interior of the State of New York. A military company were desirous of presenting their captain with a testimonial of their approbation of his services as a soldier and a man, for, as one of the resolutions expressed it, "he was always foremost in the hour of danger," meaning, I suppose, that he had had the temerity to stand within six yards of the target on one of their excursions. A silver cup was purchased, and it was presented in the following fashion:

"Captain," said the gentleman honored with the duty of making the presentation, "Captain, there be the jug."

"Ah," said the Captain, "are that the jug?"

"It are," was the reply.

"Nuff ced," exclaimed the Captain, "and now let us liquor."

Mr. Hill left New York in the packet ship Oxford, Captain Rathbun, in the month of August, 1836. Among the passengers was the Hon. Charles A. Murray, now Master of the Queen's Household. He was returning from his tour through the United States, the particulars of which he has given in a very impartial and entertaining book of travels. He formed a very sincere attachment to Mr. Hill, and took every occasion during Mr. Hill's residence in England to evince the deep interest he had in his success.

Mr. Hill was the life and soul of the party on board, and they used to assemble in the cabin of an evening, and listen for hours to his amusing stories. The following relation was delivered on one of these occasions :—

"Ike Marble came driving the Deacon's mare along one day, like nothin ! 'Well, Sol,' says he, 'yer goin' to uncle Ephs ?' 'Why,' says I, 'I ain't fixed up nor nothin'.' 'Jump in,' says he, and he took me by the coat-collar, and pulled me in kerchunk. Away we went : we skipped over the airth like real tearers ; pretty directly we brought up to uncle Ephs, all standing like an empty bag full of nothin'. Well, in I goes into the parlor and sot myself down right alongside of uncle Ephs' Betty. Says I, 'Betty, how d'ye due ?' I couldn't git along a bit though, for she blushed just like a blue carrot. Presently in come Nancy Slocum, Ike Marble, and a hull lot more of gals and fellers. By jingo, I never seed the like afore, and there was I settin' right in the wrong place, for the gals all seemed to take a taring liking to that room. Bime by, Nance says, 'Sol, will you go in t'other room.' Confound it, thinks I, you got another room ? Howsomdever I did go in, and arter a little while supper was got ready, and I took my stand right behind the door so as to see the gals as they went out by one room into t'other; presently somebody said, 'Better shut the door tew;' slam went the door. 'Boo!' says I, and they all cried out, 'Why, Sol.' They opened their mouths wide enough to swaller a haymow. At last I got sot right down between Nancy Slocum and Sal Barton, with a large chunk of pumpkin-pie in one hand, and Nancy's hand in t'other. Just as I was goin' to ask Nancy if she loved apple sarce, in comes Ike Marble with his white trowsers all daubed with mud; it sot me a larfin so, right afore Sal Barton tew, that I dropped a great junk of pumpkin pie right slap on Sal Barton's new gown: then sich a time: Sal jumped up, Ike looked blue, Nancy blushed, and I sneaked out. Oh! I swow if I ain't one of the most unlucky critters that ever breathed. Tryin' to git out of the way, I went into uncle Ephs cupboard and sot myself slap down in one of aunt Nab's custard puddings. Oh, dear! as I was fumbling round to git out, down come a bottle of pepper-sarce into nine hundred pieces. 'Mercy!' screamed Nancy, 'what's in our cupboard?' The door flew in and I flew out, all dripping with custard, bang agin Nance, chunk agin Sal Barton, out through the porch, and over the bridge, as if Satan was arter me, and if you catch me there agin you'll catch a white weazel asleep, I tell you."

During the passage across the Atlantic, Messrs. Murray and Hill used to issue a daily paper, which was a source of infinite amusement to the little public of which they were the head and front. I regret that I have it not in my power to present several numbers of this Atlantic Journal. The following communications appeared in one which has been preserved:—

"BERTH LODGE, STEERAGE COUNTY,
"August 27th, 1836.

"*Messrs. Kinderer, Murray, Hill & Co.*,

"GENTLEMEN:—Ever since I moved into this country, I have been very much interested in the case of an unfortunate woman who resides in my vicinity. She is daily pining away, without any disease that medical skill can detect. When I first knew her she was almost a skeleton: she has now but a thin transparent covering to her bones. The sight of her has been so piteous as often to take away my appetite, especially when the vessel works and rocks more than usual. She refuses all consolation, and has never, till this very day, made any disclosures of the sercet of her suffering. Yesterday morning, as I was reading the Last Breeze, I was startled by a sudden scream; I looked up and saw her falling, while No. 4, who had evidently been talking with her, was endeavoring in vain to support her; she fell senseless. We used water, Cologne, &c., while Doctor Lobelia was sent for, but all our efforts and his were ineffectual. The hottest steamings produced no impression upon her. We were giving her up as a gone case, the only case he had ever lost, the Doctor said, when she had revived enough to say, 'Oh Sol;' but instead of proceeding in her Latin invocation to the sun, as we supposed it, she fell back, became drowsy, and slept till this morning. The Doctor seeing that nothing more was to be done for her at present, first asked me if he should look to me for his fee, then discoursed upon the blessings of the Thomsonian practice; then took the two Latin words she had uttered as a theme for a phrenological harangue to the audience, which had now gathered round him. 'Only think,' said he, 'of Latin from a woman of her condition, how wonderful !' 'You, none of you understand it, but I do. I see it in her eyes; only look, how prominent,' for in truth her flesh had fallen away so that they stood out like goggles. But I ought not to repeat his discourse, which was so eloquent, that the audience upon the spot formed a phrenological society, and voted to request a copy for the press; you will, no doubt, be applied to to print it. This morning the poor woman seems quite bright and has applied to me to write to you in her behalf, as she is not able to write herself. Her yesterday's emotion was occasioned, she says, by hearing from No. 4, that a man had been seen in your country calling himself Solomon, and mentioning her name with Sal Barton. She has no doubt but that it is her sweetheart, Solomon Snifflenose, the deacon's son, and as her life depends on his being found, she wishes you to advertise him in your extensively read and highly valued paper.

"Your friend and subscriber,

"ZERUBBABEL SKINNER.

"P. S.—I enclose an advertisement and a letter for Mr. Snifflenose, should he be found.

"LOST, STRAYED, OR STOLEN,

"A first-rate Sweetheart, 27 years old, 5 feet 4 inches in height, weighing 149 pounds. He has a round faee, lips that turn up most bewitchingly at the corners; is a charming little fellow every way, and answers to the name of Solomon, or, more commonly, Sol Snifflenose. I have no money, but any one that will give me information where said Solomon may be found, will do more than I can tell, for a distressed maiden; and if any person will seize him and fetch him right to me, he shall have the first cent I find in the ashes

"Witness, "Zerubbabel Skinner.

her
Nancy ⋈ Slocum.
mark.

"N.B.—He must be treated kindly.

"Dear Sol,—I take my pen in hand, or rather Mr. Skinner (don't squint, Sol, he is 50 years old, and has got a wife and children), takes it for me. I'm in such a taking, Sol, I can't write to inform you that I am in good health, and hope you enjoy the same blessing—(Mr. Solomon, I, the penman, Z. Skinner, must interrupt the course of the epistle, to say that this is a lie, told so as not to hurt your feelings; she is as sick as she can be and live, and is dying to see you.) Oh! Sol, what a spot of work you made when you run into that closet and then run away from me. Oh! dear, dear! did you know, Sol, what tender affections you were crushing in the bud, you'd never have sneaked out so, after having thrown so many sheep's eyes, and a squeezing my hand, so as eenmost to make the tears come. What if you did sit down in mother's pudding? 'twas clean dirt; and if you don't like the cow's milk you need not kill the heifer calf to spite her. Oh! I shall die, Sol—(a sigh here as long as your father's nose, Mr. Solomon.—Z. S.) if you don't come back. When you run I took arter you as you'd a seen if you'd look back, but I might as soon have thought of catching a weazel, or legging it arter a streak of lightning. I went home, but I could not eat any more than our white pig, when the black one had rooted his trough over. So, one night, I took a bundle of clothes and sot out, to see if it I could not find you. I heard you were seen on your way to New York. I followed on, and who should I see, as I was trudging down Broadway, with the houses on both sides as thick as Sue's pumpkins, but Jerry Snaggers. He told how you were going to old England, and he guessed as the great folks there would snicker well to see such a sloony of a Yankee among them. I wanted to pull his whiskers for him, but, says I, 'twon't do here 'fore folks, and asked him how you were going? He said he did not know, but a new ship was jist on the start and if I went in it I should be sure of getting there as soon or sooner than he, so I looked as pleasant as a basket of chips and asked him to go with me to get on board: so we went; and the Captain asked me whether I would go as a cabin or steerage passenger? 'Which gets there first?' says I, 'Why there ain't much difference,' says he, 'but if without we back in the steerage folks have a little the best chance,' so I took his advice and went right aboard. I've looked for you ever since and axed some sly questions for you, but till just now, (the poor woman has no idea of the lapse of time, Mr. Snifflenose.—Z. S.) I've supposed you were in some other ship. Oh! Jiffins, how Bill made me jump. I thought I should have gone out of my skin. And now I'm in sich *pewter basin.* But do come and see me, Sol. You will, won't you, Sol? Don't say you won't, Sol; now, you won't, Sol, will you? Your best friend,

"NANCY SLOCUM.

"She cried so here, that she could not tell me anything more, and as the mail is just going she wants me to put down her name and send it off. Yours, &c.,

"Z. S."

Mr. Hill arrived safely at Liverpool, and after a short stay there, proceeded at once to London.

We may regret as much as we please that we have not more independence of judgment on this side the Atlantic than to be influenced by the fiat of a London audience in dramatic affairs: it is nevertheless true that we are so, and all the regrets and sarcasm in the world to the contrary, it will have weight among us. Mr. Hill was fully impressed with the important bearing his success or failure in London would have upon his fortune in the United States, and this added to the doubts and fears which every actor would feel in appearing before a strange audience, made him excessively nervous and anxious about his appearance. The Yankee dialect was but little, if at all, known in London; and he knew that his success must depend on something more solid than the mere delivery of quaint sayings in a strange and peculiar dialect. Mr. Hill, in contemplation of the hazard he was running in venturing upon entirely new ground before a British audience, often had his misgiving upon the propriety of the step he had taken. At home, he stood alone the representative of the Yankee character; he was applauded to the very echo wherever he appeared, and not a theatre in the Union which was not open to him whenever he chose to engage: but he felt, that if he failed in his present enterprise, his brilliant prospects at home would be, if not entirely blighted, at least materially dimmed.

Mr. Hill was engaged by Mr. Bunn, then lessee of Drury Lane, to appear at that establishment. Mr. Bernard, the well-known dramatic author, was employed by Mr. H. to prepare a new piece for his debut. The Yankee Pedlar was the result, and in this piece Mr. Hill made his first bow to a British audience. Mr. Price, the able partner of the late Edmund Simpson, Esq., was exceedingly kind to him, and did and said all he could to encourage him. A few days before he appeared, Mr. H. received the following note from Mr. P.:

"My dear Sir: I understand you have been very much annoyed by some remarks of Mr. Bentley's. It was certainly bad taste in him to mention to you his dissatisfaction, which I presume arises from the part assigned him. You are to remember you want all your nerve, and I am quite sure you may depend upon a warm reception. Go on, fearlessly, and you need have no dread of the result. You will have many warm friends in the house who will support you. Yours, truly, S. Price."

The eventful evening at length arrived. Public expectation had been much excited by the novelty about to be presented for its enjoymnnt, and the house, on the evening of Mr. Hill's appearance, was full of the fashion and beauty of London. He was received with the utmost enthusiasm, for there was that in the manner of his entrance which at once impressed upon the minds of the audience that a genuine artist had made his entrée. How well he succeeded may be seen by the following notices which appeared in the London papers.

Mr. Hill thus wrote to his friend Woodworth:

"London, Dec. 12, 1836.

"My dear Woodworth: I was most happy to receive your kind favor bearing date Nov. 16th, but grieve to hear that you have been so afflicted with your eyes as to cause your resignation at the 'Navy Yard, Boston.' Before this can reach you, you will have heard of my success at

'Drury Lane,' which was most triumphant. Cordelia (I believe) has a letter from me, which contains the account of my first appearance here, which I have no doubt she will read to you. I am pleased to hear you have done something more for the American Drama; let authors and actors work for each other in our beloved country, and the time is not far distant when we shall build a dramatic fame among us, which will be the envy of the world. I am so much engaged at this period, that I cannot give you as long a letter as I wished, but promise one when I am more at leisure. Remember me to your family, and believe me, as ever, Your sincere friend, G. H. Hill."

"*S. Woodworth, Esq.*"

From the London Times, Nov. 2, 1836.

"Drury Lane Theatre.—One of the most curious and novel representations that our stage has seen, was exhibited last night, in the performance of Mr. Hill, an American comic actor. Mr. Hill, it seems, has been extremely popular in America, for the humorous fidelity with which he has portrayed the characteristics of Yankees, a race whose peculiarities excite no small degree of mirth among the nephews and nieces of Uncle Sam. The sketches of the late Mr. Mathews and the lucubrations of Major Downing and Colonel Crockett, have given us some notion of the oddities of the down-easters. Mr. Hill's personations furnish a finished picture, of the accuracy of which we have no reason to doubt, and of the whimsicality of which we readily bear witness to. But the true merit of his acting is, that he gives a perfect picture of a very odd character hitherto very slightly known on our stage, and proves in that power of humor which is somewhat rare and always highly attractive, he can fairly take his stand among the best low comedy actors we possess. He was received with great applause, his jokes produced abundant laughter, and the audience seemed so to relish the whim of the representation, that he can hardly fail to become a favorite. He was called for, after the close of the piece, and his announcement of its repetition was received with universal approbation. Some more such importations as Mr. Forrest and Mr. Hill, and our dramatic freights to America will be brought much more directly under the reciprocity system than they have hitherto been."

FROM THE LONDON GLOBE, OF NOVEMBER 2, 1836.

"DRURY-LANE.—Mr. Hill, who has obtained pretty considerable celebrity in America, by his droll performance of Yankee characters, last night submitted his pretensions to the approval of a London audience, who were highly amused with his quaint humor, and awarded him a hearty welcome, and applauded his exertions as vehemently as the most ardent of his countrymen could desire; the audience seemed fully determined to prove how happy they were to acknowledge talent from wherever it might come, 'and went the whole hog' in expressing their approval of the 'stranger's' talents. A new 'local' and characteristic sketch, in one act, entitled 'The Yankee Pedlar; or, Old Times in Virginia,' was prepared for Mr. Hill's appearance. It is from the ready pen of Mr. Bernard, and, as a *piece de circonstance*, merits commendation. Its leading incidents serve to portray the peculiarities of that portion of our trans-Atlantic brethren termed 'Yankees,' or in their expressive vocabulary 'Down-Easters.' Mr. Hill sustained, in the piece, the part of Hiram Dodge, a Yankee pedlar, a counterpart of our 'canny Yorkshire lad.' Not finding a market for his razors, which he assured his customers, if oiled, and put under the pillow at night, would astonish the buyer, who would find himself clean shaved when he awoke in the morning, he becomes successively a servant, a confidant, a carpenter, and jockey, with a view to gain unappropriated dollars, and is at last brought upon the stage defunct, having been thrown from a horse in a race; he, however, revives with alacrity, upon hearing his *quondam* master exclaim, he would give forty dollars if he were alive again, and clenches the offer at the instant. The principal attraction and peculiarity of the performance was the quaint, dry humor of the actor, and the many odd phrases and similes interspersed throughout the dialogue. At the conclusion of the piece, Mr. Hill was liberally applauded by the audience, and called forward to receive the expression of their approbation."

FROM THE LONDON TRUE SUN, NOVEMBER 2, 1836.

"DRURY-LANE.—Our heart always warms to an American in England: still more to an American on the English stage. We went prepared to greet Mr. Hill with cordiality, and predisposed to be pleased. We need not have fostered a friendly feeling towards him. He had not been ten minutes on the boards ere he had deserved aud commanded it from every man, woman, and child. There is a *bon-hommie* about the man, which attaches one to him before one has had time to appreciate his original and very effective powers of humor. He was very diffident on his first appearance, and never perfectly gained confidence. His manner of mingling gravity and grins is irresistibly comical. 'His smiles,' aptly observes a brother critic, 'are like fits of sunshine on a cloudy day.' A Yankee pedlar is a hybrid animal, of a class so thoroughly indigenous, that none but a Yankee of native acquaintance with its characteristics, could meetly personate its peculiarities. This, Mr. Hill, we rather imagine, did for the first time last night. He is a valuable addition to Mr. Bunn's corps. When called for at the close, his heart was evidently full. We have witnessed 'a return thank' speech from a countryman of his, to which Mr. Hill's *uncalculating* and *heartfelt* incoherence presented an admirable contrast."

FROM THE LONDON CHRONICLE, NOVEMBER 2, 1836.

"Drury-Lane.—The entertainments at this theatre last night, besides the Siege of Rochelle and Der Frieschutz, (two full-grown operas, a musical repast more than sufficient for the most voracious appetite,) consisted of 'a local characteristic sketch, in one act, called the Yankee Pedlar; or Old Times in Virginia.' This is evidently a genuine American production; and it served, too, to bring before the English public another American actor of merit. We cannot describe Mr. Hill in this part farther than by saying that in aspect, gait, dress, language, and dialect, he completely realizes the conceptions we had previously formed of the singular race whose representative he is. Some of his Yankeeisms were beyond our conception, but the picture altogether was delightfully quaint, humorous, and witty; and the audience showed their relish of it by incessant laughter and applause. The plaudits at the end of the piece were prolonged till Mr. Hill made his appearance to make his acknowledgments."

FROM THE LONDON COURIER, NOVEMBER 2, 1836.

"DRURY-LANE.—Last night, an amusing trifle, called The Yankee Pedlar, introduced a Mr. Hill, a transatlantic brother, to a London audience. The story turns upon a peddling body (Mr. Hill), who introduces himself, by means of an intercepted letter to one Colonel Bantam, a fowl-breeding, horse-rearing, Virginian planter, as a jockey to ride in a match pending between the Colonel and a friend. Having made his way into the Colonel's house, he begins to mend the furniture, play the spy upon the daughter and her lover *incognito*: takes money of the last not to discover him to the father, and finds it equally worth his while to break his contract. Meanwhile, the fraudulency of his intrusion is discovered, and he is entrusted with a note to the Colonel's slave-driver, which is intended to procure him a small amount of lashes; but he discovers the intention, gives the responsive to the original bearer of the introductory letter, and offers to ride for the Colonel's antagonist. The Colonel's horse is rode by the young lady's lover, to whom the Yankee pedlar loses the race, and the winner is rewarded with a wife. The honest pedlar is full of Yankeeisms, colloquial, moral and gesticulative, which lose none of their point in the hands of Mr. Hill. The new actor is of an agreeable appearance; he is slight in figure with a particularly-pleasant countenance, and a pleasant smile, as far as the very confined nature of the part allowed him, Mr. Hill displayed great humor and animal spirits. He was cordially received, and his agreeable address soon made him friends with the audience."

FROM THE LONDON JOHN BULL, NOV. 6th, 1836.

"At DRURY-LANE, they have received another 'help' from America. Tragedy and comedy have both visited us from beyond the Atlantic; it is but just to the actors to state, and also to the public, that their reception has been honorable to each. Mr. Hill, as well as Mr. Forrest, has established his reputation in his own country; his experiment, also, as to how far John Bull would sanction the verdict of Brother Jonathan, has been satisfactory to him. We are glad of this; our own players have, in general, met with fair and liberal treatment in the States, and it is pleasant to return the compliment. The peculiarities of the 'Yankees,'—a class, and not the people of the United States,—have been already rendered familiar to us. Mathews took them off, and so did one of themselves, two or three years ago: Mr. Hill comes to England for the express purpose of furnishing us with his 'notions' of their oddities, and does it with irresistible humor and effect.

He plays at Drury-Lane, the part of a Yankee Pedlar, a sleek, plausible, laborious, and enterprising rogue, with a dialect and phraseology to be found universal among his fellows, but nowhere else in the world.

"Of such novel *materiel* Mr. Hill makes a great deal. Every word he utters tells: and the audience roars duriug the whole of the time he remained upon the stage. We 'guess' he will 'do,' also, in other parts; and cannot fail to be a favorite in all."

FROM BELL'S NEW WEEKLY MESSENGER, NOV. 6th, 1836.

"DRURY-LANE.—Another actor from America, made his bow to an English audience, at this theatre, on Tuesday night,—a Mr. Hill, who is said to enjoy considerable reputation in his own country, as a representative of 'Yankee characters.' A new farce, written by Mr. Bernard, was produced on the occasion: its title, 'The Yankee Pedlar,' Colonel Bantam (Mr. Bartley) has a daughter Nancy, (Miss Lee,) whose hand he is anxious to bestow upon a friend; but the young lady prefers a lover of her own choosing, and befriended by Hiram Dodge, the pedlar, (Mr. Hill,) she prevails upon her father to consent to her union with her favorite. Mr. Hill's dry humor amused the audience greatly; and his Yankeeisms created much laughter. At the conclusion of the performance, Mr. Hill was called before the curtain, when he proceeded to express his thanks for his reception, in a speech evidently *not* 'made for the occasion;' what he spoke came from the heart, and we were too well pleased with the manner, to quarrel about the matter of the speech. The other characters, mere make-weights, were as well supported as it was necessary they should be."

FROM THE LONDON COURT JOURNAL, NOV. 5th, 1836.

"MR. HILL, an American actor of the comic cast, made acquaintance with a London audience, on Tuesday night, in a local sketch, called the Yankee Pedlar, a broad farce. The Yankee Pedlar manages to make his way into the house of one Colonel Bantam, (Bartley,) where he intrigues and tricks some fifty or sixty dollars into his pocket, by playing spy upon the Colonel's daughter and her lover, —hiring himself to the latter as confidant,—and jockeying the Colonel into winning a horse-race against his own arrangements, and giving his daughter to her lover against his will.

"Mr. Hill is slight in figure, pleasant in countenance, with a most agreeable address. He laughs, turns grave, is bustling, lounging, solemn, and chattering, by turns. All the versatile knavery of the Yankee, with his undeviating eye to the main chance, he pictures in right lively style. Before the piece was over, he and his audience seemed to have grown quite familiar; and being called on at the end of the piece, in accordance with a silly custom, he expressed his deep sense of the kind welcome he had received, in just so many words."

FROM THE LONDON SATIRIST, NOV. 6th, 1836.

"The next that we have to notice, is Mr. Hill's performance of the Yankee Pedlar, in a sprightly and well-written piece of that name, from the pen of Mr. Bernard, the author of a variety of dramatic pieces, among the rest, that of the Nervous Man. Mr. Hill is an exceedingly clever actor; his style is of the most quaint and quiet description: he embodies a picture of a thorough-bred Yankee, who succeeds only by a sly and fraudulent cunning, in the most humorous manner possible. He has already become a great favorite, and as characters are capable, as we have seen, of being written for him here, we 'guess' that his stay with us will not be very short."

FROM THE SUNDAY EVENING GLOBE, NOV. 6th, 1836.

"DRURY-LANE.—Mr. Hill, another American performer, in a line totally different from that of Mr. Forrest, made his appearance at this theatre on Tuesday. A local sketch called 'The Yankee Pedlar,' was the vehicle of Mr. Hill's peculiar talent, and it is but justice to say, that it was developed very cleverly. Everybody has been amused at one time or other, by Yankee exaggerations, delectable in their very extravagance; in this 'sketch,' there is a choice 'batch' of them, delivered in the genuine racy style of a 'native.' Mr. Hill's humor is unlike anybody else's that we have seen; it is as quiet as it is quaint and felicitous, and bears the strong impress of truth. He is the smoothest and slickest of pedlars, lies with so much ease and comfort, and overreaches with such sly satisfaction, that we are glad to make his acquaintance. He, in short, gives an exceeding diverting picture of Yankees and Yankeeism, and if he play as well in his future characters, as in this, he will always receive, as he did on his first appearance, a warm welcome.

FROM THE LONDON SUNDAY TIMES, NOV. 6th, 1836.

"DRURY-LANE.—We have this week to record the appearance of another American actor of fair promise, on these boards, in the person of Mr. Hill, who had previously acquired considerable celebrity in all the principal American theatres, by his representation of "Yankee characters," a line of business that is somwhat synonimous to our Yorkshire country boys. We have hitherto been accustomed, not ill-naturedly, we trust, to confound everything American, by the general term of 'Yankee,' but this is quite a mistake. As in England, all rustics are not York, so in America, the same class are not all 'Yankee.' It is a distinct *caste*, peculiar to the eastern states, and like our Yorkshiremen, is chiefly distinguished by shrewd cunning, under the mask of simplicity. Mr. Hill made his debut before an English audience, in a farce called 'The Yankee Pedlar,' which Mr. Bernard has so adapted to the British stage, as to render the main features of the principal part, tolerably intelligible. At this moment, we cannot call to recollection, any character of our own drama, which bears sufficient similitude to it, to afford room for comparison; but though wholly unacquainted with the original, we may imagine the portrait given by Mr. Hill, to be a faithful one. The piece is plentifully interlarded with local witticisms, and is altogether a very agreeable bit of broad comedy. Hill's acting was easy and natural, sufficiently comic to keep the risible muscles of his auditors in constant play, without any straining at effect. The Americans call him 'little' Hill, and so he is; but his figure, though not colossal like Forrest's, is well formed and his features are good, and capable of the richest comic expression. Though he had not quite so much to do as we could have wished, he has certainly made a most favorable impression by his performance, even of this trifling part. Bartley's Colonel Bantam, was an exceedingly happy conception, and it was equally well embodied. In parts of this description, Bartley has no rival. At the fall of the curtain, there was an universal call for Hill, who came forward and expressed his acknowledgments in modest, but appropriate terms. The farce was given out for repetition amid loud plaudits.

FROM THE LONDON MORNING HERALD, JAN. 4th, 1837.

"OLYMPIC THEATRE.—Last night, Mr. Hill, celebrated throughout the United States of America for his correct personation of the Yankee character, made the second appearance upon these boards in his original part of Hiram Dodge, in Bernard's farce of 'The Yankee Pedlar.' Having fully detailed the plot and incident of this trifle when it was some short time since produced at Drury-Lane Theatre, it would be a work of supererogation now to do so;—we have, therefore, but little to remark upon the present occasion, further than to record its success here, as well as the favorable reception of Mr. Hill, whose performance was honored with great and frequent applause. The manner of Mr. Hill is perfectly quiet, and his acting more nearly resembling that of the late "little Knight," as he was called, than any we have since seen; and his stories, for which his countryman has contrived this farce as the vehicle, are not unlike in their quaintness, humor and minuteness of detail, though, of course, far exceeding it in the *romance* peculiar to the new country, that of "Betty at Heckleton Fair," which all who have heard it from the lips of the latter, must well remember. The size, therefore, of his present arena, is peculiarly adapted for Mr. Hill's performance, as it enables *all to hear*, and hearing, few failed to laugh outright. The piece was in other respects, well supported, and had, in addition, the advantage of new and appropriate scenery.

FROM THE LONDON SUNDAY TIMES, JAN. 8th, 1837.

"OLYMPIC.—Mr. Hill, the American comedian, whose successful appearance at Drury-Lane in the Yankee Pedlar, we noticed some weeks back, has been enlisted into the ranks of the Widow of Wych-street. Mr. Hill appeared here on Monday last, in the same part, and has played each succeeding night with increased applause. His quiet humor tells better than in the larger house—at all events, he contrived to keep the audience in roars of laughter, during the whole of this performance

(Mr. Hill was acting at this period, at Madame Vestris's and the Queen's Theatre, every night.)

FROM THE LONDON MORNING POST, JAN. 10. 1837.

"QUEEN'S.—A new piece entitled Caspar Hauser, or The Wild Boy of Bavaria, was produced last night at this theatre. We understand it is written expressly for the purpose of exhibiting the peculiar powers of Mr. Hill, whose delineations of Yankee character are very amusing and racy. The plot is founded upon a story which made much noise about five years ago, but which eventually proved to be an imposture. The writer of this piece, however, takes the story for fact, with the only alteration of conducting it to a happy catastrophe. The piece told well; most of the pictures and positions were very effective; the scenery was good; and (as the loud applause which followed the falling of the curtain, testified) the play was decidedly successful. Dr. Lott Whittle, the character enacted by Mr. Hill, was admirably adapted for the exhibition of those national peculiarities in which that gentleman is so successful. He is well described by one of the *dramatis personœ* as an "anythingarian"—a sort of Yankee Caleb Quotam, with the same variety of calling, but more quickness of resource and a harder intellect. He describes himself well, when, in answer to the question of "where he took out his Doctor's degrees," he says, "I did not do it by degrees; I jumped into it at once." At the fall of the curtain, Mr. Hill was unanimously called for and loudly cheered.

FROM THE LONDON CHRONICLE, JAN. 11, 1837.

"QUEEN'S THEATRE.—A new piece entitled 'Caspar Hauser, or The Wild Boy of Bavaria,' was produced on Monday at this Theatre. The plot is founded upon a story which made much noise about five years ago. The piece told well, and was decidedly successful. Dr. Lott Whittle, the character enacted by Mr. Hill, was admirably adapted for the exhibition of Yankee peculiarities, in which that gentleman is so successful. At the fall of the curtain Mr. Hill was unanimously called for and loudly cheered."

FROM THE LONDON DAILY ADVERTISER, JAN. 11, 1837.

"QUEEN'S THEATRE.—On Monday evening, Mr. Hill, the American Comedian who has acquired so much celebrity in Yankee land, made his first appearance at this heatre. The piece, however, which is purely of the melo-dramatic school, had been got up with the utmost care and attention to scenic effect, and it proved exceedingly attractive and successful. The chief star of the piece, which seemed to have been written entirely for his introduction, was Mr. Hill, who personated Dr. Lott Whittle, a kind of nondescript comic creation, framed for the purpose of delineating the Yankee countryboyism. This gentleman's style of acting is exceedingly modest, and we can readily believe true to the life. He strains not an atom, but speaks his author, as the original would do. This may not at first take the fancy of every one who associates the idea of comedian with something very much out of the way; yet we were pleased to see that the audience were caught by his style, and were exceedingly liberal in their applause. At the conclusion of the piece, the expression of approbation was tremendous; and it ended with Mr. Hill being under the necessity of presenting himself before the curtain. His Americanisms were really very quaint and amusing.

FROM THE LONDON TRUE SUN, JAN. 11, 1837.

" Queen's Theatre.—Mr. Hill, the American Comedian, appeared at this theatre last night, in a new piece called 'Caspar Hauser, or the Wild Boy of Bavaria.' Mr. Hill sustains the part of Dr. Lott Whittle, an everythingarian; but particularly great in medicine and painting. Those who have read Lord Stanhope's interesting account of Caspar Hauser's imposture, for such it was at last discovered to be, will find that the actual circumstances are followed pretty closely in the drama. He is made, however, to be the lost heir of a noble family, his uncle being the Baron Rhemfelt (Mr. S. Johnston.) The Baron has an only daughter, Eva, (Miss Clifford,) who discovers the wild boy in his loan retreat. She saves him, and leads him into the haunts of men, and has him carefully educated. They become mutually attached and are to be united, when Caspar is stabbed by a villain named Grippeswald (Mr. Reed,) who aspires to the hand of the young lady. The murder is discovered through the agency of Dr. Lott Whittle, and the piece concludes. Miss Grey sustained the part of the Wild Boy with considerable ability, and contrived to make him a most interesting person. The chief burden of the piece, however, fell on Mr. Hill's shoulders; but he seems to delight in such difficulties, for he kept the audience in constant laughter. The humor of his new character, is broader than that of the Yankee Pedlar, and we thought that Mr. Hill seemed to enjoy the fun of the part in a higher degree. He sang two songs very humorously, and showed that he knows well how much may be gained by keeping back a talent until the proper moment arrives for its display. There is one particular in which Mr. Hill has no rival—and that is his manner of telling a story. He introduced several last night, and the effect was irresistible. The piece was much applauded, and was given out for repetition amidst loud acclamations. Mr. Hill was called for after the fall of the curtain.

Mr. Hill afterwards played in all the principal towns of England, Scotland, and Ireland, and in every place received the enthusiastic applause of large and brilliant audiences, attracted by his name and fame. During his sojourn in Great Britain he made many valuable friends. His engagements, however, were of too pressing a nature to allow him much time for social pleasures. The following familiar and friendly letter from the Honorable Mr. Murray, will serve to show how difficult it was, at this time, to put a finger upon Mr. Hill.

"LEAMINGTON, Feb, 23, 1837.

"MY DEAR 'BLOWHARD:'—I am really vexed at the obstinate pertinacity with which a certain 'gentleman in black with a forked tail' seems to contrive that we should never meet, although both are in this little island; for, no sooner do you move to the north, than I am carried off to the southern districts, and your letter has *hunted* me from Dunmore Park to Oxford, thence to London, and thence to this place, where I am sojourning with my mother, who is an invalid, and drinking the mineral waters of this Spa: and now, as your letter is dated the 13th ult., I know not where mine may overtake you, or whether it will ever reach you at all, as you seem to be on a flying tour, of which I know not the ultimate destination; but I will address it to Edinburgh, and merely assure you of my sincere regret that our house should be empty, and all the family absent, while you are in the neighborhood; it has been but a sad and melancholy dwelling since my poor father's death, but you should have had a bottle of good Madeira, and a hearty welcome; and you shall still have both, if you will visit us in the autumn, when the families are all at their country seats; whereas you are rambling through the country, when every soul is in London, attending the court and the parliament. Pray let me hear something of your proposed movements, and let us see if we cannot induce the gent in black to allow us to meet somewhere to have a few hours' chat about Johnny Wrath and his merry crew. Believe me very sincerely yours,

"Charles A. Murray."

"To G. H. Hill, Esq."

Mr. Hill was in Edinburgh when he received the foregoing letter. The following extracts from the Scotch papers sufficiently show how highly he was appreciated in the "land o' cakes:"—

FROM THE EDINBURGH SCOTCHMAN, FEB. 15th, 1837.

"THE THEATRE. Mr. Hill, the celebrated American comedian, and personator of 'Yankee country boys,'—as the play bills have it,—commenced a short engagement here on Wednesday evening, in the character of a 'Yankee Pedlar,' an odd mixture of shrewdness, wit, and cool impudence, in the representation of which Mr. Hill displayed a degree of talent which shows him to be an actor of considerable 'mark and likelihood.' His line of character is some degrees below the highest on the stage; but, nevertheless, there is no want of room in that line for the display of good acting. What we admire most in Mr. Hill, is the admirable command which he seems to possess over his comic powers. He does not throw away his efforts upon so many separate and unconnected 'hits,' or exhibit any haste to distinguish himself all at once; but, repressing and bridling in his piquant humor, he pursues 'the even tenor of his way,' chastely and quietly, trusting not to petty details, but, as the poet says of beauty, 'the joint force and full result of all,' for the admiration and applause of his audience, which here, at least, has been accorded to him most warmly. The representation of Yankee character, besides, is new to us in this quarter; and the very novelty has a charm in it, which recommends his acting to our liking. We have only yet seen him in this one part; but we understand he is no less excellent in the only other character in which he has as yet appeared,—'Zephaniah Makepeace,' a down-easter out of place."

FROM THE EDINBURGH CALEDONIAN MERCURY,
FEB. 16, 1837.

"Last night Mr. Hill, the celebrated American Comedian, whose representations of Yankee clowns have been so attractive in London, made his first appearance here and was very warmly received. We were glad to see this generous feeling evinced towards a stranger, because, whatever may be our partiality to native talent, it shows that a Scottish audience is always ready to acknowledge merit, apart from all such extrinsic considerations. The present actor has the advantage of presenting to the British public a *genus* quite unknown in our dramatic literature, and, of course, the novelty would of itself go far to heighten the attraction; but Mr. Hill has no need to rest his claims on this circumstance, as his own comic talents afford a far more secure basis. The piece chosen for this occasion was termed the 'Yankee Pedlar,' being a local sketch of American manners, though the other characters are entirely subservient to that of the Pedlar, who by his roguery or address contrives to bring his fortunes to a successful consummation. Mr. Hill performed the Pedlar, and, as far as we could judge, it seemed a most natural representation—our opinion being confirmed by several who are acquainted with the peculiar manners and eccentricities of the lower classes in America. His style is eminently chaste, bearing some resemblance to that of Irish Power, who figures in a different sphere. Mr. Hill does not seek to overpower his audience by any wild freaks or sallies, but he attains his end far more effectually by a chaste, quiet, but yet easy and flowing vein of humor. In short, often when appearing to do nothing he does everything, if we may so express ourselves. In several scenes he was much applauded, particularly in one, where a Planter, having written a letter to his overseer, and dispatched the same by the Pedlar, with his instructions to give the bearer 100 lashes, the Pedlar, with an intuitive caution, which seemed his *forte*, peeped into the fatal mandate, and seeing its contents, dexterously selects another bearer. He afterwards rejoins the Planter, who, confident of the success of his stratagem, eyes his man with amazement on hearing him ask, with a cheerful countenance, if he had any farther commands. He was met, however, by a look from the Pedlar equally knowing and expressive, which convulsed the house with laughter, and evidently showed Mr. Hill to be an actor. At the close of the performance the applause continued long and loud, until at last Mr. Hill made his appearance, and with great good taste simply confined himself to announcing the piece for repetition. We feel confident that the public will avail themselves of this opportunity of witnessing this actor in a new and interesting field of dramatic adventure."

FROM THE EDINBURGH COURANT, FEBRUARY 16, 1837.

"THE THEATRE.—Last night Mr. Hill, an American performer, who has acquired considerable celebrity in this country by his delineation of American manners and peculiarities, appeared, for the first time in Edinburgh, in an admirable farce, entitled "The Yankee Pedlar." Mr. Hill, of course, sustains the principal character; and the quaint simplicity of his appearance and deportment, the amusingly cool self-possession with which he pushed forward his own interests, his quiet humor, and his sly sagacity, told with irresistible effect on a very numerous audience. His engagement, we observe, is announced for only eight nights, but we are sure his performances will become so popular as to induce the manager to extend it."

FROM THE EDINBURGH OBSERVER, FEBRUARY 17, 1837.

"Wednesday Evening, Mr. Hill, the American Comedian, came before the Edinburgh audience as 'The Yankee Pedlar.' He was received with enthusiastic courtesy, and in a few minutes established his claim to approval. His appearance is prepossessing, and his countenance (and his eye especially) expressive of sly humor—and, without meaning anything offensive, assuredly, to his national feelings, we may say he presented, in the shape of the Pedlar, some of those traits which we should guess belong to that class in Yankee land, an order who can take gain in the form of money from opposite parties, and 'then stand upon principle.' His performance throughout was 'tarnation' and 'cantankerous' clever, and kept the house in an unceasing convulsion of laughter. Without the aid of prophecy, we venture to predict both the piece and the performer will be prodigious favorites among us. When it was finished, there were loud and continued peals of laughter and applause, indicating that he was called for, and another member of the corps who came forth to announce a repetition (we suppose) having got a hint to retire, Mr. Hill re-appeared, and intimated that 'The Pedlar' was to be produced the following evening. The announcement was received with loud plaudits. Mr. Hill is evidently a first-rate performer in his walk, evincing the most perfect ease, and that semblance of nature which, without serving effort or art, is, in reality, an achievement of the highest art.

FROM THE EDINBURGH EVENING POST, FEB. 18, 1837.

"THE THEATRE.—Mr. Hill, the celebrated American comedian, has been with us during the week. His chief walk is the down-easter, or regular Yankee, a character *sui generis*, and well worthy of a representative on the stage. Mr. Hill seems to have studied the class most perfectly; at least we can have no doubt of the natural effect of his performance. Nothing could appear less of a caricature: and yet he renders the character most entertaining. His performance proves him a first-rate comic actor, in some respects not inferior to Liston, of whom he strongly reminds us. The dialect of Yankee and peculiar slang of the tribe are conveyed with most amusing effect by Mr. Hill: but perhaps the richest part of his performance is the droll impudent *stare* which he assumes when he wishes to be perfectly and particularly *slick*. Altogether, we consider Mr. Hill's personations capital embodiments of character, only less laughable because they bear the stamp of truth. We should say that we have few comic actors on our stage to be compared with him."

FROM THE EDINBURGH OBSERVER, FEB. 21, 1837.

"Mr. Hill continues to delight, by his masterly delineations of the Yankee character. If ever there was a man of talent in his art, it is this American. He has the finest and most expressive eye that ever spoke more eloquently than words; he is gifted with a taste and discrimination which never allow him to exaggerate, even where that were pardonable; and, to use a low term, very well understood in high places, however, there is no *humbug* about him."

FROM THE EDINBURGH JOURNAL, FEB. 22, 1837.

"Mr Hill, the American comedian, has been engaged for a very few nights, and takes his leave on Tuesday. We regret his departure, and hope it may be postponed. This clever actor introduces us to an entirely new line of characters,—for the Yankees of the stage have been, hitherto, mere caricatures, while Mr. Hill's performances are finished pictures, bearing the impress of nature in every line. His rich and inexhaustible humor is never obtrusive, and the quiet way in which he goes on developing the character, without the slightest straining after 'making a point,' resembles the style of Keeley and Irish Power. Like the latter, too, he is a capital hand at telling a long story in a way which keeps one's attention unweariedly on the stretch. He has a fine, good-humored face, and a capital voice. We have been delighted with the little we have seen of him;

and should like much to see more of him than his engagement, (if unextended) will admit of.

"On Tuesday, Mr. Hill takes his benefit, when, if the favor he meets with is proportioned to his merits, there will not be an empty seat in the house."

FROM THE GLASGOW COURIER, MARCH 9, 1837.

"THEATRE ROYAL. Since our last notice, Mr. Hill, the American, has been increasing in attraction, in the character of Hiram Dodge, the Yankee Pedlar. He has also sustained, with equal success, another character, but nearly of a similar nature in all its essential features, namely, Dr. Lott Whittle, an 'American travelling artist of all work,' in a melo-dramatic piece, entitled 'Caspar Hauser, or the Wild Boy of Bavaria,' in which Mr. Hill has greater scope for the development of his Yankee peculiarities. In it no point of any consequence was omitted: it was a full embodiment of the character, and left nothing farther to be desired. His humor was inexhaustible; his style of acting inimitable."

His last engagement in Scotland was in Glasgow. As the time grew near for the termination of his European tour, he became more and more anxious about home, and was impatient for the day to come when he should leave the scenes of his triumph, for the more solid joys which awaited him at his fireside. The letter which I give below, addressed to Mrs. Hill from Glasgow, will express his feelings at this time, much better than I could give them:

"GLASGOW, MARCH, 1st, 1837.

"MY LOVE;—Having a few spare moments, I will occupy them by writing once more to thee. I have just laid down my flute, after playing '*Home, sweet home,*' and oh, how that air comes *home* to my feelings now. Though a few days will find me embarked for my native land, it appears that the time never passed so heavily, and I must repeat once more, that if my God will suffer me to meet you again, we will not separate, till one or both shall be called to another world. I was, last night, dreaming of you, and that you clung to me in an hour of deep distress: I partly awoke, and turned to speak to you, and say it was but a dream, but found no one near me. I was alone, in a melancholy, cold room, and naught to cheer me but the moon's rays. I arose from my bed, put on my morning gown, and sat by the window, I should think, an hour.

'Silent I gazed on the midnight sky,
  While sad was the spell that bound me,
The pale moon shed, from her arch on high,
  The gift of her glory around me.'

"I made my first appearance here on Monday last: the house was full, and my reception as warm and enthusiastic here as in Edinburgh. I play here ten nights. I've been buying you some Scotch presents, to-day, which I think you'll be pleased with. Tell the children that father will not forget them; they shall have some delightful presents when I return. I have many engagements offered me now, but having made up my mind to sail on the 20th, or 24th inst., have been obliged to refuse till I return. Do take good care of yourself and children, and pray fervently, as I do, that my journey may be a safe and speedy one to the bosom of my dear family.

"Yours, as ever, fond and true,

"G. H. HILL."

"To CORDELIA HILL, God bless her."

Mr. Hill sailed from Liverpool in March, 1837, in the ship United States, Captain Holdridge. On his homeward passage, as he had been when outward-bound, he was the life and soul of the "goodlie companie." On his arrival in New York, he was immediately engaged by Mr. Simpson to make his first appearance after his trip to Europe at the Park. On this occasion, he appeared in a piece called "The Pedlar,' the same which was written for him by Mr. Bernard, and played with such success in England. His reception was of the most enthusiastic and flattering kind. The house was crowded from pit to dome, and when he made his entrée, it was many minutes before he was allowed to speak, for the applause which greeted his return. He played to overflowing houses every night of his engagement. In the month of June he visited Louisville. This was about the time when that disastrous re-action took place, which followed the speculating epidemic of 1835 and '6. Whilst he was in Louisville, the following lines appeared in one of the daily prints of that city:

"In these dull times of care and sorrow,
When tribulation fills each breast,
When every merchant dreads the morrow,
And notes and protests haunt their rest.
Nature ne'er made a mortal fitter,
The worried heart with joy to fill,
Than that delightful, humorous critter,
That soul of frolic *Yankee Hill*.

"Others may strut with tragic brow,
In tragic tones their grief make known,
Such serious themes don't suit us now,
Wit we would have, not fun alone.
A Yankee Pedlar opes his pack,
Of recipes each care to kill,
In Louisville, there is no lack
Of friends, to welcome *Yankee Hill*.

"Where'er he travels, east or west,
O'er rugged roads or stormy waters,
No favorite e'er was so caressed
By wit's gay sons and bright eyed-daughters.
When souls with welcome mirth are gushing,
And Fancy's sparks with rapture thrill,
When the full founts of wit are rushing,
Be there to charm us, *Yankee Hill*"

He next appeared in Cincinatti; he was a great favorite in the Queen of the West, whose citizens always assembled in crowds, to welcome his appearance among them. He played a short engagement next in Boston, and then re-appeared at the Park in New York. He was advertised to play Solomon Swop in "Who wants a Guinea," but Mr. Hackett placed an injunction upon the Theatre. The injunction was, however, soon removed, and Solomon Swop made his bow with the more unction after the initiation into the mysteries of the Court of Chancery. Solomon, although threatened with a *suit*, did not get into any of the *bad habits* usually acquired by gentlemen of the long robe.

He then went to Philadelphia, and from thence to Washington. He was here an accredited Ambassador from the Court of Momus, and right welcome was he in a place where motley is so much the wear. Men worn out with the ponderous duty of making laws, or jaded with the more arduous task of feathering their own nests, or making new ones for their friends, were glad to turn aside and enjoy the pleasant entertainments offered by Mr. Hill. The farces annually played in Congress, are only entertaining to the players engaged, being altogether what actors call "too talky for the mass." These beside, being monstrously expensive, are got up with such an utter disregard to place, unity and time, that it is a wonder almost, the managers have not shut up the Theatre long before this, and put the performers to some more congenial employment.

Mr. Hill was always successful in Washington, for his entertainments were of a character to attract the attention of the best people there. I have now before me complimentary letters from Mr. Clay, John Quincy Adams, and others, all expressive of their appreciation of Mr. Hill's talents as an actor. Among the incidents and anecdotes related in another part of this book, will be found a speech delivered by Mr. Hill, on the Oregon question, so that it will be seen, that whilst he had an eye to maintaining the humor of his country, he had a most patriotic regard to the other great interests of the land. After putting matters right in Washington, he returned to New York, which place he left in a few days, to fulfil an engagement at Albany. On his voyage up the North River, he was seated in the cabin reading a newspaper, when he observed an odd-looking individual reading over his shoulder. Mr. Hill looked up in his face, when the fellow, with his hands in his pocket, and not in the least disconcerted at being caught in so impertinent and unmannerly an act, exclaimed " Any news in particular ?"

" No sir ; will you accept the paper ?"

" Oh no, can't ; ain't got time. It's the first time I've been up this River, and I want to be looking reound. How can they take a fellow up this river for a dollar and found. They can't dew it. It's a take-in."

" How is that ?"

" Why they charge one dollar to take you in, and when you git up to Albany, you've got to pay another dollar to get eout. Got this place all fixed up so. Sophy's all reounu tew. I never use Sophy's myself, but once courted a gal by that name, and it looks a kind o' natural to see Sophy's reound ; and them stuffed-bottom chairs eout there. I thought I'd set deown on one on 'em ; by thunder, I jumped up three feet. Oh, I'll be darned if I didn't think I was sitting down on sombody's baby. You see I chaw tobacco ; grandfather chawed, and father he chawed, and mother, she—eh—no, she didn't, she snuffed, so you see I have to keep running up to expectorate—as our doctor says, overboard. I expect I shall have to go again in about a minute."

" You need not take that trouble, sir," said Mr. Hill, " here are spittoons."

" Spittoons ! Oh, yes, I know'd what them was for, but they've got 'em brightened up so, I didn't like to nasty 'em.

I went to the The-ater to see you t'other night. Didn't you see me? I sot right in front of you."

"No, sir, I did not."

"Wal, I don't suppose you could; there was a hull lot of fellers there. I got jammed in. I had on a striped vest, the fronts were new, but the backs being made of cotton, sometimes will give eout. By golly, I got .tew laughing, so away went the back, slitted right up to the collar. I was a little the tornest critter you ever did see."

"I am very sorry for your misfortune," remarked Mr. Hill.

"Oh, you needn't fret abeout it, Mr. Hill. I shouldn't a wore it much more nor three weeks longer, anyhow. You see I never wear my best clothes to sich places, 'cause it kind a rips them eout a leetle. I had a bet abeout you, Mr. Hill. Some feller said you was born on Long Island. I told him you wasn't, you was born down-east."

"You were right, sir, I was born in one of the eastern States."

"There, I know'd you was, 'cause I know'd you couldn't get along so well as you did, if you wasn't born deown that way somewhere. Have you been in Massachusetts?"

"Yes, sir," said Mr. Hill.

"Been in the State of Maine?"

"Yes, sir."

"Been in New Hampshire?"

"Yes, sir."

"Ah. Maybe you was born there? They've got a good many Hills."

"No, sir, I was not."

"Wal, you might have been. Ever been in Vermont?"

"Yes, sir."

"You know old Zeke Hill?"

"No, sir."

"Nor I nuther, but I've hearn tell there was such a feller, didn't know but you might have known him tew."

"Have you ever been in Connecticut?"

"Yes, sir."

"Ever been in Rhode Island? that little bit of a thing in there."

"Yes, sir."

"Have you ever been in Boston?"

"Yes, sir."

Having thus obtained nothing very satisfactory from Mr. Hill, in relation to his birth-place, he commenced asking him if he had been to the Capital of this State, and then the other, until he had got through the whole of them; he then, to Mr. Hill's astonishment, commenced with the country towns, doubtless with the hope of hitting at last upon the one in which Mr. Hill was born. Mr. Hill, getting a little out of patience, said, "I presume, sir, you wish to ascertain where I was born?"

"Wal, yes, I shouldn't mind knowing, if you have no objection to tell, and if you had told me before, you would have saved me a darned sight of trouble."

"Well," said Mr. Hill, "I was born in Boston, in the year 1809, on the 8th day of October, at six o'clock in the morning."

"At six o'clock, eh?"

"At six o'clock precisely, down in Water street."

"Dew tell. But Mr. Hill, *dew you remember the number of the house?*"

This was carrying inquisitiveness to the very extreme, and would have been very annoying to any man but one engaged like Mr. Hill in enlarging a gallery of odd pictures.

After finishing his engagement at Albany, he went to Boston. He was next to play at Baltimore and Richmond; he deferred the latter engagement, however for a time, in order to play for a complimentary benefit tendered to his old friend and author, Samuel Woodworth, Esq. The benefit came off at the Bowery Theatre, and resulted in the substantial gain of $1500 to the beneficiary. I am told by those who were present on this interesting occasion, that he never played so exquisitely before. Every look he gave, every word he uttered, told with immense effect upon the charmed audience. My informant remarks, that he seemed almost inspired. Knowing as I do, the benevolence of Mr. Hill's heart, I can readily understand the inspiration he felt, for he knew that the poet's heart would be made glad by the results of his exertion, and it threw a spirit into his acting, which mere personal gain could not have done. Mr. Hill was at all times ever ready to assist the needy and deserving in his profession. He appeared for benefits time after time: often with great inconvenience to himself, and almost always with a loss in a pecuniary point of view.

After the benefit, he proceeded to fulfil his deferred engagements at Baltimore and Richmond. He was very much dissatisfied with the company at the latter place, for they were not only deficient in dramatic ability, but also in respectability of character, and nothing was more galling to Mr. Hill than to be obliged to appear with persons of this description.

In the month of December, 1837, he went to New Orleans. Several incidents which occurred to him in that city will be found in another part of this work. Mr. Hill, during this visit labored under a nervous depression, that rendered him very miserable. He felt so depressed at times, that it was with difficulty he could be urged to play at all. Sometimes, even when dressed for a part, he has wished to give it up, and would on many occasions have done so, if he had not almost have been pushed upon the stage by the Manager. It is a singular thing, that the moment he came in view of the audience, he seemed a changed being, and not a soul in front who looked upon his laughter-provoking face could have believed for a moment, that he was the wretched being he really felt himself. This state of health continued upon him for some time; so bad did he feel, that when, in a short time afterwards he was playing in Philadelphia, he always had a physician with him to feel his pulse and look at his tongue every time he came off the stage. To those who are unacquainted with the witch-like character of a nervous affection, this may appear almost incredible, but any one who has suffered from a similar affection will readily sympathize with the sufferings he felt.

Mr. Hill was now preparing for his second visit to England. He played a farewell engagement at Boston and in New York, and on the 26th of May, 1838, sailed for Liverpool, in the packet ship Sheffield, Captain Allen. Mrs. Hill accompanied her husband on this occasion. In nineteen days from the time of leaving New York, Mr. Hill and lady landed in Liverpool. He lost no time in that town, but as soon as his luggage could be got through the Custom House, proceeded to London. He was engaged at the Haymarket Theatre, and made his first appearance, after his return, in the comedy of New Notions, playing the part of Major Enoch Wheeler. This piece ran with great success for one entire month. He played for two months at the Haymarket, and then went to Edinburgh. He was a great and deserved favorite in Modern Athens. Mr. Hill's health which had been much improved by the sea voyage began to suffer somewhat from his residence ashore, but his spirits were better, nevertheless, than they had been before leaving home, for Mrs. Hill was with him to cheer and sustain him with her attention and affection. He left Edinburgh and sailed for Dublin. He caught a severe cold immediately on his arrival in Ireland, so that on the first night of his appearance he was scarcely able to make himself heard. He soon recovered from this and made himself heard to great advantage, for few strangers have appeared on the Dublin boards who gained warmer friends or left behind a more pleasing impression. During his sojourn in Dublin, he made an excursion to a country town, a few miles from the city, for the purpose of picking up odd notions for future use. He attended a meeting which was called together for the consideration of the propriety of building a new jail. Mr. Hill made note of the following items.

"*Resolved.*—That a new jail shall be built on the same spot on which the old one now stands." (*Carried unanimosuly.*)

"*Resolved.*—That, for the sake of economy, the materials of the old jail should be used in the construction of the new one." (*Carried.*)

"It was moved by the Rev. Mr. Phalem, that for fear the prisoners should escape, that the *ould jail should not be taken down until the new one was built.*"

Mr. H. next appeared in Liverpool, then at Nottingham and Birmingham, and in each place won fresh laurels. In the inside of the coach which Mrs. and Mr. Hill took at Birmingham for Nottingham, was a fine, portly old dame, whose conversational spring seemed to have been wound up and warranted not to run down, until everybody else was. She was scarcely seated in the stage when she commenced by addressing Mr. Hill, thus:

"Sir, do you know Mr. S———?"

"No, madam."

"Dear me, why I thought everybody knew him! He is brother to ———, who married Mrs. G.'s daughter; very respectable people in Birmingham; and there is Mr. A., he has a son in the army, a wild young man, although I suppose—black moustaches—you have never—dark, curly hair—seen him?"

The old lady waited for no reply, either from Mr. or Mrs. Hill, but ran on:

"This is a beautiful country along here," she continued. "That is the seat of Lord ———; splendid place, is it not?"

"Yes, madam."

"He married Lady ———, and they say she is not so happy with him as she would be with some other person. I don't know, myself, but people will always have so much to say. Strange thing, people will talk, talk, talk; for my part, I can't see the sense of it. What a fine child you have. Is that your child, sir?"

"Why, madam, the belief that I am the father of my own child, is one of those romantic sources of mundane pleasure that I fully indulge in at the present moment."

"Yes, sir, no doubt. Look here, pupsy-tupsy, look at

this picture. I stop at Higby; I have friends there, and my house is not far off. Where do you go, sir?"

"To Nottingham, Madam."

"Nottingham is a fine town, sir?—is it your home?"

"No, madam."

"You go there to see friends? Have you ever been on the railroad?"

The coach suddenly stopped at an hotel, when the old lady left the stage and met an acquaintance with whom she shook hands, and immediately opened her lingual battery. Just as the coach was leaving, the old lady toddled up to the coach door and called out to Mr. Hill, "Sir, sir, I may want to speak of you to my friends; will you be so kind as to give me your name." Before a reply could be given, the four spanking bays of the road had separated the parties for ever.

Mr. Hill returned to London, to play a short engagement previous to his departure to France. There appeared in one of the London papers, an article, which Mr. Hill thought reflected a little strongly upon his countrymen, and he addressed the following note, which the Editor had the fairness to publish.

"No. 5, Tavistock Row, Covent Garden.
Dec. 17th, 1838.

"Sir:—I find in your paper of yesterday, an article which speaks of me as the 'representative of the peculiarities of my countrymen.'"

"Now I beg to state, that I only profess to give, what I know to be a faithful picture of the rustic '*Down-easter*,' the '*Yorkshireman*' of America, as they are sometimes styled. As it regards a *gentleman*, they are the same in all countries: and neither '*Hiram Dodge*' the Pedlar, nor '*Major Wheeler*' of the Penobscot Militia, have any pretentions to such a title. Yours, respectfully,

"G. H. HILL."

Mr. Hill, having obtained his passports, proceeded to Paris. This trip was undertaken more for the benefit of his health, than for any professional purpose; but there were in Paris a great number of English and American residents, who insisted upon his giving a few entertainments. They could not think of allowing him, of whom they had heard so much, escape them, without his giving a touch of his quality. The following letter addressed to Mrs. Hill, who remained in London, speaks of his arrangements.

"EVER DEAR CORDELIA:—I am in Paris, and have made arrangements to act at the theatre where the English Company played, and have the favorable opinions of all as to the success of the undertaking. I was very sea-sick crossing from Dover to Calais, and strained till I brought up some blood, which alarmed me very much. The journey in the coach fatigued me, so that I am not myself exactly yet, but hope to be in a few days. The moment I commence operations, you shall hear from me again (God willing.) Write often to me, for a favorable line from you will keep me in spirits.

"Yours, sincerely, fond and true, G. H. HILL."

"Jan. 23d, 1839."

Mr. Hill, gave two entertainments in the French Capital with eminent success. The French critics, although, perhaps, scarcely comprehending the humor of the down-east phraseology, saw in him and so esteemed him, a Comedian of rare endowments.

During his sojourn in Paris, he attended a Masquerade Ball, in which he appeared in his favorite Yankee character. It is customary at these entertainments for the masquer to reveal his face before entering the room. Mr. Hill, in obedience to the rule, took off his mask; he had scarcely shown his face when some person cried out "Why, Yankee Hill;" and his hands were instantly seized and almost shaken off from his body in the excessive joy of the person who had so quickly recognized the American Comedian. There is something deliciously pleasant in these unexpected meetings, thousands of miles away from home, even where the parties in their own land were not very intimately acquainted with each other, as was the case here. The gentleman who so cordially took Mr. Hill by the hand, had never before exchanged a word with him, but he had sat many an evening at the Park Theatre and enjoyed his company with *unspeakable* delight, and he thought this fact, and the magical name of *countryman*, was justification enough for exercising the privileges of a friendly recognition. When the stranger left America, Mr. Hill was playing at the Park, and he was not aware of his visit to Europe until he saw him under the circumstances I have just related. Among the stories, collected by themselves in another part of this book, will be found a sketch of the American Political loafer. I give below, one of a French loafer, whom Mr. Hill met in Paris.

Of all characters well calculated to excite the risible faculties, and appeal to the sympathies of the human heart, beyond doubt it is the unfortunate and destitute Frenchman. There is such a mingling of the gay and cheerful, with the sombre and melancholy, and so rapid are the changes of feeling, that it is not wonderful, if we have sometimes thought the French people as shallow and superficial in feeling, as they frequently are, in what are called accomplishments. But amid all the privations to which the Frenchman may be reduced, his motto seems to be ' nil desperandum." I once encountered a Frenchman of this character in Paris, and amid the glitter and festal blaze of that theatre of fashion, he seemed as lonely as some mouldering ruin of past centuries amid the gaudy architecture of the new world. Said he,—" No sar, I sal not take any charitie, but I will tell you what I will go do. I will go by ye river, and jump myself in, and they sal see me no more nevare. But, poor Marie! No! no! I sal do no such sing. I sal no kill myself, for she sal then starve; but, Monsieur, I sal starve myself, and I sal live starving, and Marie sal fare magnifique, and I sal live starving to be happy, and see her live as well. No, no, I sal no kill myself."

In two hours from that time I met him again, his countenance wearing a smile of almost cheerfulness, apparently having satisfied himself with the uncomfortable philosophy of going without eating.

The French loafer in this city is, perhaps, after all, of a higher class than we have ever mentioned. He saunters along by himself, looking the picture of despair; he neither solicits alms, nor does he complain to all. He has apparently made up his mind for his fate, and alternating between despair and brightening hope, he lingers out his career until relieved by the charity of others or by death.

The French loafer, by choice, is to be found in the

billiard room,—the Café,—the Saloon, and but too often in the halls of our fashionable citizens, who, sometimes, with a desire to improve acquaintance, and appear somewhat more aristocratic, endure the burden of their company, fascinated by that most magical and meaning word a French Count. The first-mentioned lives at the billiard table; he is usually an expert player, or, in other words, a blackleg; and can win or lose as it suits the purposes of the game. He has usually a large dark eye, extensive whiskers, and hair hanging down over his neck of the most glorious description. He utters more "Got dams" and "sacré dieus" than would set up a whole committee of politicians for twelve months. The last-named order of loafer, is the especial delight of ambitious mothers with marriageable daughters, and the daughters, perhaps un-unwilling to thwart the benevolent intentions of their mammas are fascinated by the "dear, delightful Count," until some sensible brother, or upright, honest father, finds the said Count to have been an impostor, and, after a few parting hysterics, surrenders the toy, and wonders they "ever could like him."

Before leaving Paris, a public dinner was tendered Mr. Hill by his friends and admirers, and they included some distinguished French gentlemen, almost all the American and English residents, then sojourning in the gay capital. Mr. H. with health improved and in gay spirits, returned to London to fulfil an engagement at the Haymarket. He opened on this occasion with a new piece entitled a "Wife for a Day," written expressly for him by Mr. Bernard. The play was eminently successful. On the first night of its representation, Mr. Hill was called out, and he announced the repetition of the piece every night until further notice, amidst the cheers and applause of the gratified audience. It ran without interruption for an entire month. Whilst in London this season, he produced Seth Slope with success. Mr. Hill paid £30 sterling for this, but for each of the pieces written for him by Mr. Bernard, he paid forty pounds, or about two hundred dollars. In the summer of 1839, Mr. Wallack, the manager of the National Theatre, of New York, visited England, for the purpose of obtaining attractions for his establishment. He met with Mr. Hill in London, and over-persuaded him to accept a starring engagement at the National. He was announced at that establishment among the attractive stars secured by the manager, to the great gratification of the play-going public. He now completed all his arrangements, and left England, in the British Queen. The late Mr. Price came passenger with him, and, during the passage, used all his rhetoric to induce Mr. Hill to engage for the Park, but without effect. Mr. H. fulfilled his engagement with Mr. Wallack, much to his own misfortune and loss, as it eventuated, in consequence of the destruction of the National by fire. After playing his term at the Park, he appeared in October, in Boston, where he was received, after his absence, with the utmost enthusiasm. He left, after this, for Philadelphia, and returned to Boston again in December. Mr. Hill used to relate with great unction, the well-meant, but equivocally expressed good wishes, of an Irishman who used to make the fires in his room at the hotel. Mr. H. had been in the habit of giving little presents and orders to the theatre to his good-natured attendant, which won his heart. He made him such tremendous fires, that he almost roasted him. When Mr. H. was leaving the Tremont House, the Irishman was very officious in helping the porter with the luggage. When the luggage was all arranged in the coach, and Mr. Hill was seated, ready for the start, Pat raised his cap from his head and exclaimed, "Good-bye to ye, Mr. Hill—long life to yer honor; I hope I shall have the pleasure of making fires for you *hereafter*."

In the Spring of 1841, whilst in Boston, he appeared as Richard, in a burlesque on the tragedy. In the last scene, the person playing Richmond accidentally gave Mr. Hill a severe blow upon the face. Thinking he was seriously injured, he rushed from the stage: the prompter met him at the side and said, "Mr. Hill, you did not die." He returned immediately, and said, "Ladies and gentlemen, I beg pardon; I left out an important part of the piece; I have quite forgotten to die." He then took up a violin, and playing a simple tune, laid himself down and died, as calmly as though nothing had occurred to interfere with the peace of his last end. How common it is for men, playing on the stage of real life, to forget the dying scene, notwithstanding the promptings so plainly, forcibly, and frequently given. The audience, on the occasion I have just related, had too much of a fellow feeling in this forgetfulness of death, to feel aught but good humor at the ready manner in which Mr. Hill repaired his error.

Mr. Hill was one of those few fortunate men who were in the possession of a happy fireside. No matter what distance his duties may have placed him from his home, what success crowned his efforts, what attractive gaieties may have gained his passing admiration, his face always turned to his own hearth, the East of his adoration. In reading his letters to his wife, bearing dates from the period of his first professional absence from home, to the time when his fatal sickness seized him, I have been struck with the almost romantic attachment which they exhibit towards the partner of his bosom. No professional triumph or success seemed to be complete until Mrs. Hill had marked them with her approval, and no disaster could long depress his spirits when the smiles of his wife and children, and the cheerful influence of his own fireside, were within reach of his enjoyment.

Mr. Hill's home feelings never deserted him through life: his attachment to his wife and children knew no abatement. He was gifted with an uncommon flow of animal spirits, and he took as much delight in projecting little entertainments for his children, or winning a laugh from his wife by some grotesque assumption of character, as he did in laboring for the amusement of the brilliant audiences which assembled to witness his efforts.

In writing the biography of a man, the task is but half completed if only the great points of his career are recorded. In circumstances likely to come under public notice, men are on their guard, and act with caution. We can judge of the ability of an actor on the stage, but it is behind the scenes that we must go to study the character of the man. To say that Mr. Hill was a great comedian, that he personated this or the other character with exquisite truthfulness, only excites the curiosity of the thinking, to know how he appeared, acted, thought and spoke when he was himself. The world is very apt to think and do as the countryman, who, when thrown accidentally in company with a celebrated actor, asked him "to be funny," and was wonderfully disappointed to find that the comic actor had his serious and thoughtful moments.

In all that related to the higher duties, which devolve upon a father towards his children, Mr. Hill was seriously impressed. Their moral and intellectual education received an attention commensurate with its importance, and although he would often enter into their sports and entertain them with odd personations and imitations, they knew very well no license, if unseemly, or disobedient conduct could be drawn from this.

In a profession surrounded with such temptations to convivial enjoyment, as is that of the actor, Mr. Hill must have been more than human, if he could at all times have avoided a participation in them. An attendance upon public festivities and private parties are among the sacrifices which an eminent actor must make ; and I have often thought, that too little allowance is made for the apparently gay life the actor sometimes leads, considering the urgent demands continually made upon his time and company. An actor lives upon the approbation of the public, and although he may desire to live in private ever so much, he must take the public by the hand, off as well as on the stage ; and he is thus, perforce, compelled to submit to pursuits and pleasures foreign alike to his tastes and inclinations. Mr. Hill, would, at all times, if left to his own selection, have preferred the quiet joys of his own fireside to the most sumptuous entertainment ever offered for his acceptance.

The approbation of his wife was to him a *sine qua non* to every novelty he intended to produce before the public; and, when on the first trial of a new entertainment, he had Mrs. Hill among his auditors, so placed, that he could see her, he was perfectly happy if she seemed pleased and entertained. Had Mr. H. been any other sort of man than what he was,—if you please, dissipated, thoughtless, gay, —the satisfaction he felt, simply from the approbation of the partner of his life, displayed an integrity and soundness of heart which would safely guard the fireside from the invasion of evil influences.

Mr. Hill was very fond of taking his family by surprise after an absence, and would sometimes appear at the door of his dwelling so disguised, that even his own children knew him not. He used to tell an incident of this kind with great relish, because, in this case, he not only deceived his children, but his wife, and this was a triumph not to be held lightly. He went down town one evening, on some business, which detained him until after dark. When he reached his home he gently opened the door with his latch key, closed it and stood quietly in the hall. It was but the work of a moment to disarrange his dress, crush his hat down upon his head, and assume the reckless dishabille of a drunken man. He then made some sort of noise to call the attention of the family to the fact that some one was there. Mrs. Hill sent her little boy to see who was at the door. It was but a minute, and the little fellow returned in alarm, telling his Ma, that there was a drunken man standing in the hall. Mrs. Hill, her servant girl and the children were alone in the house, and as drunken men are not apt to be over nice and delicate in their conduct, it will be admitted, that such an intrusion was well calculated to produce alarm. A council of war was held for a moment, and it was resolved, boldly to face the enemy. Female arms are the most powerful weapons in the world in the wars of love and friendship, but they are powerless in defensive attacks, so that it was deemed prudent in the present instance that the alarmed family should die, at least, with harness on their backs, and each seizing upon the family arms, represented here by shovel, tongs, poker, broom, &c., the army marched up stairs to the attack. Mrs. Captain Hill courageously led the way: she was the first to mount the stairs from the basement; on reaching the top she paused to collect her forces: this done, she marched boldly on, resolving to do or die. It was no false alarm; there, sure enough, stood the enemy. The foe was struck with amazement at the belligerent attitude of his own household, but unable longer to resist the ludicrous position of his family, he burst out laughing and declared himself vanquished. Arms were recovered, and all joined in the mirth inspired by the trick.

It would be a tedious as well as unprofitable pursuit, to follow Mr. Hill through the various stages of his theatrical career, after his return from England, to the time of his decease, although embracing a period of nearly ten years. He appeared, again and again, in all the principal cities of the Union, pausing occasionally at some country place, generally at the earnest solicitation of the inhabitants, to relieve the tedium of their country-town life with his eccentricities and drolleries. For several years, dating from 1840, theatrical affairs throughout the whole Union were in a very depressed condition. The re-action which followed the excitement caused by Fanny Ellsler, the ruin produced to managers by a persistence in the starring system, the lecture and concert mania which prevailed for several years, all tended to depress dramatic affairs. From 1840 to 1845, Mitchell's Olympic was the only theatre in the city of New York, in a prosperous condition. The Park opened and closed with convulsive efforts at re-animation, until it fell, exhausted by its own efforts. It passed from the hands of Mr. Simpson, who had controlled its fortunes for nearly thirty years, into the hands of Mr.

Hamblin, who, in his turn, was relieved of its weight by a fortunate accident, which burnt down the house, without burning his fingers. Mr. Hill appeared occasionally in this city during these times of depression, and with quite as much, if not more success, than other stars who appeared at that period.

In the years 1844 and 1845 he resided in Fourth Avenue, near Union Square, New York. Returning home one evening very late, after performing, he was startled by the sobs of a female he saw sitting on the stoop of a house, close by where he was passing. She was weeping bitterly. He was not the man to pass heedlessly along, leaving a fellow-creature by the wayside in trouble, without making an effort to allay, or to relieve it. He questioned her of the cause of her distress. She did not seem disposed to reply, until, at length, overcome by the kind tones in which she was addressed, told her sad, but, alas, too common story. She had been enticed to the city by a treacherous villain, under a promise of marriage. He took her to a house of infamy, on their arrival in the city, and left her there alone, promising only to be absent long enough to transact some necessary business in another part of the city.

Ere he came back, the poor girl had learned the character of the house in which her deceitful lover had left her. Without waiting his re-appearance, and without the knowledge of the degraded inmates of the house, she made her escape, and had been wandering about the city until Mr. Hill, fortunately met her. He himself was a father, and with a father's care conducted the poor wanderer to his own dwelling, where she received, in the kindness of Mrs. Hill, another evidence that the race of good Samaritans is not quite extinct in the world. The next morning Mr. Hill sent the girl home to her parents, who were residing in Middletown, Connecticut.

On the 1st of January, 1847, Mr. H. gave an entertainment at the Broadway Tabernacle, to a very large and brilliant audience; numbering, as I am informed, about three thousand persons. In the opening of the same year, he went to Batavia, N. Y., to fulfil a contract made between him and a gentleman of that town, for the country-seat now occupied by the widow, Mrs. Hill, and her interesting family. The last theatre in which Mr. Hill appeared was Mitchell's Olympic. He played a starring engagement here of twelve nights, drawing excellent houses. I saw him several times on this occasion, and thought I had never seen him play with more freshness and spirit. During the last twelve months he employed his time professionally, in giving lectures here and there, returning as often as he could to his house in Batavia, loaded with golden profits. He was essentially a domestic man, and never was so happy as when in the midst of his family. Without any pharisaical ostentation of religion, Mr. Hill was careful to inculcate in the members of his family a due observance of their religious duties. There are a great many *unchristian* professors of Christianity, who are unable to reconcile, in their austere and contracted minds, the existence of a religious sentiment with the pursuits of the actor. They judge him as they themselves would not like to be judged, viz. with the mask on. They do not follow the player to his home, and watch him in the bosom of his family. They take no count of the private bending of the knee, the humble supplications which he offers at the footstool of God's Almighty throne, but taking him as he appears in the midst of his vocation, fling him to perdition without hope or charity. I do not claim for Mr. Hill that he was what is appropriately enough, I think, called a *professing* Christian, that is, he did not

> "Display to congregations wide
> Devotions every grace, except the heart;"

but he was a practical one in charity and good feeling towards his fellows. He had, besides, a sustaining confidence in the providence of God. No trouble ever weighed upon him, but he found in this reliance a cheerful hope of speedy relief. This feeling, whether a superstition of religion, rather than a principle evolved by a reasoning faith, always kept him up in the hour of trial, and consoled him under every difficulty. This feeling grew with his growth, and, during the last few months of his existence, he was seriously impressed by his spiritual condition. Whatever appeared in his entertainment, which could, by any possibility be construed into anything offensive to the purest taste, was carefully excluded, and he even went so far as to ask several eminent clergymen, if they saw anything in his entertainments, "*contra bonos mores.*"

In May, 1848, Mr. Hill appeared in Brooklyn, before immense audiences. He was always a favorite in that city, and ever attracted the best people of the place. In the summer he played also at Sharon Springs, and then in August, visited Saratoga for the purpose of lecturing to the fashionables collected there. He was taken sick soon after his arrival. He had advertised to appear on a certain evening, and, although it would have been better had he broken his faith in this case, and nursed himself up for future labors, he could not make up his mind to do so, and after consulting his physician, who consented to the step, he left his sick bed and proceeded to the lecture room. He was behind the time advertised for his commencement, and when he entered he was greeted with marked signs of disapprobation. He mildly rebuked the audience, by explaining the cause of his detention, and more in sorrow than in anger, remarked, that in the course of his varied career, he had often waited with patience for an audience, but he had never till this moment kept an audience waiting. The audience felt the rebuke, and with ready contrition, cheered and applauded him then and during the whole evening. How little do the audience know, or even care, for the suffering which the actor sometimes endures, when he is most successful in contributing to their enjoyment. The bills of the day are out, the theatre is filled with beauty and fashion, and the entertainment must come off though the principal actor may be tortured in body, ready to sink with sickness, or perchance, as I have known, torn from the bedside of a sick wife, or dying child, to fret his hour upon the stage, convulse others with laughter, whilst his own tortured heart was swelling with agony, almost to bursting. Mr. Hill left the lecture-room for his bed, from which he never rose again in health. He was ailing for some time before his symptoms became so alarming as to render it necessary to send for Mrs. Hill: at length this became necessary. She received the sad missive, and hastened to the couch of her beloved husband. Her presence was so inspiring in its influence upon him, that there seemed a distant hope that he might yet rally and be restored to her; but alas ! such hopes speedily vanished and gave way to the solemn conviction that his battle of life was fast drawing to a close. Mr. Hill himself had been for some time under the impression, that he should not live long, and when he was attacked with the bilious diarrhea, he never flattered himself with the hope of recovery. The Rev. Dr. Milledolar payed him frequent visits during his sickness, in fact, was daily with him until his death. Mrs. Hill never left his bedside for a moment, and frequently, when the labor of speaking was too much for him, would he turn his still sparkling and expressive eye towards her, and in looks, tell of the love and affection of his heart. He retained the full possession of his senses until a few hours of his death. The sad, awful moment at length arrived, when the ties which bound him to this world were to be unloosed, and the spirit set free. Mrs. Hill sat by his side. He appeared to be calmly sleeping. A soft smile played upon his lips. His breathing was gentle as an infant's. She, whose heart had known no other lord, whose affections had known no alteration save in increase of growth and strength, sat sadly by and watched his sweet and gentle slumbering, and could hardly realize that death could be so near. The lips parted, a gentle sigh escaped, and the "wheel at the cistern had ceased to turn for ever."

He died on the 27th of September, 1848, in the 40th year of his age. He was buried in the cemetery of Saratoga. The Rev. Mr. Babcock, of Ballston, performed the funeral ceremonies at the house, and those at the grave side were conducted by a chaplain of the order of Odd Fellows, of which institution Mr. Hill was a worthy member.

ANECDOTES AND INCIDENTS.

MR. HILL VISITS WASHINGTON.

In 1846, Mr. Hill paid a visit to Washington City. He was there during the excitement which prevailed upon the Oregon question. It would have been impossible, perhaps, for a man of much less excitable temperament than Mr. Hill, to have been in Washington at that time, and have escaped the patriotic epidemic which then prevailed to such an alarming extent. His patriotism became rampant, and he opened the flood-gates of his eloquence, and poured forth such a powerful stream, that all who opposed his views were nigh swept from the face of the earth. The speech which he made in Washington, night after night, to immense audiences, will be found carefully reported below. Daniel Webster might possibly have made a more solid speech, Clay a more eloquent one, John Quincy Adams, one more fruitful of sage experience; but neither of them. I will venture to say, could have made one quite like it. But let the reader judge for himself.

SPEECH ON THE OREGON QUESTION.

"Whoia! here I am, and intend, in a very few and expressive terms, to speak my sentiments. Mr. Speaker,

I have come all the way from Oregon, to see, in behalf of my afflicted neighbors, who live a considerable distance apart, and I want to know, what in thunder you're about here, in this comfortable location, while your fellow-countrymen, who are not allowed to emigrate north of the Columbia River, on account of a raging he-calf who is bla-ting on the other side ; but, thunder and squashes ! can this longer be borne ? No ! Can the free inhabitants, who have emigrated there with the full belief that protection was to be extended to them from the great republic, bear the yoke of British law and British tyranny ? *No, sir!* we expect you to guard us from the sneers and insults of savages, subject and give us aid, and to plant the standard of our country immutably on the 54–40, and, if anything, a leetle north. Powder and gun-flints! must we give up what is clearly proved by many of our great men—and though not set down in Webster's Spelling Book—to belong to us; will any man, who has pure American blood coursing through his veins, say, let it go, 'cause we're afraid to fight ? No, sir! no! it is not in the natur of *Liberty boys* to allow any usurpation of our rights: let us be guided by Crockett's motto, '*First, be sure you're right, then go ahead.*' I've killed four horses, worn out three pair of trousers and a pair of saddle-bags, besides spending all my money, to come here, and I must know before I go back, which way the cat *jumps*, or both countries shall hear from me, to their entire satisfaction, sooner or later. I've left my grandmother, father, wife, three children, six cows, two hosses, eighteen sheep, a gross of turkeys, geese, hens, chickens, a black dog, and a gray cat, who fondly look for my return, and I wish to know, without the shadow of a doubt, whether we are to be protected, or not, by this government, or are we tew be trampled under the iron hoofs of Europe's roaring Bull. We are strong and true at heart for our country, but we are as yet too few in number to offer just resistance. Give us a chance for a few years, however, and we will then look out for ourselves. Yet the time is not far off, when the locomotive will be steaming its way to the Rocky Mountains, with a mighty big train of cars running after it. Yes, the whistle of the engine will echo through the South-west Pass, and sharply hint to the free people of that great territory the approach of hundreds and thousands tew, who are to be their neighbors. No, sir, the time is not far distant, when our commerce with China will equal that of all the world; when the Pacific Ocean will be crossed with as much ease as the Frog pond on Boston Common. Yes, Mr. Speaker, as my eloquent friend from the Hoosier State remarks, 'Men of blood, and friends of General Washington, and that old hoss, General Jackson, I want your attention. *Lightnin'* has burst upon us; and Jupiter has poured out the Ile of his wrath. Thunder has broke loose and slipped its cable, and is now rattling down the mighty Valley of the Mississippi, accompanied by the music of the alligator's hornpipe. Citizens and fellers; on the bloody ground on which our fathers catawampously poured out their claret free as ile, to enrich the soil over which we now honor and watch with hyena eyes, let the catamount of the inner varmint loose and prepare the engines of vengeance, for the long looked-for day has come. The crocodile of the Mississippi has gone into his hole, and the sun that lit King David and his host across the Atlantic Ocean, looks down upon the scene, and drops a tear to its memory.' I am with you; and while the stars of Uncle Sam, and the stripes of his country, triumph and float in the breeze, whar, whar is the craven, low-lived, chicken-bred, toad-hoppin', red-mouthed mother's son of ye who will not raise the beacon-light of triumph, smouse the citadel of the aggressor, and press onward to liberty and glory? Wha-ah! Hurrah! where's the inimy?"

THE MUSICAL FAMILY.

In the fall of 1843, Mr. Hill was travelling one night through the woods of Georgia in a stage coach. It was pitchy dark, and the driver, mistaking the road, left the right track and upset the coach. There were quite a number of passengers, and among them a very corpulent Alabamian planter. Fortunately, Mr. Hill had matches. A light was quickly struck, and the passangers soon got out of the coach in which the shock had huddled them in a heap. The fat planter caused some little trouble in lifting out his unwieldy carcass. None of them were seriously hurt. Mr. Hill always carried a sort of medicine chest with him, and he was enabled to administer to the bruised and wounded *secundem artem.* The kindness and attention he displayed to his fellow-travellers on this occasion, so won upon the feelings of the Alabamian, that he insisted, and would take no denial, on Mr. Hill going home with him. The planter was such a good-natured, kind-hearted, jovial fellow, that Mr. Hill could not resist his importunities, and so consented to accompany him home. He was well received at the hospitable mansion of the planter. He was a widower, with a grown up son and daughter, his housekeeper, a maiden sister. The maiden sister was particularly gracious to Mr. Hill, for it was not often that a strange male *critter* found his way to their secluded fireside. In the evening, when the wine had circulated a little freely, the host proposed to have some music. "Come, sister," said he, "sing Mr. Hill, 'Is there a heart that never loved.'"

"Oh, brother," replied the ancient maiden, screwing her mouth into a pucker, and turning her head affectedly, "I really can't."

"No can'ts here, sister; you don't want Mr. Hill to find out how old you are. Come, you must sing, for I want to show him that we are rather a musical family; so come, tune up."

Overcome by her brother's peculiarly persuasive and eloquent manner, the maiden lady gave another twist of her mouth, and commenced in a sharp, shrill voice—

"Is there a heart that never loved?"

The key in which she sang, might have been the cellar key, for any resemblance it bore to anything appertaining to music. She had not sang half the first stanza, when her brother interrupted her.

"Sister," said he, "you are all wrong:—my son, see if you can succeed better."

This young man was a bony gawky, of about seventeen years of age. His voice was a mixed breed; one something between a manly bass and childish treble. He began—

"Is there a heart that never loved?"

The first three or four words were sung in a deep bass, and the rest of the line in a high tenor.

"Pshaw," said the father, "why you can't sing it either. Are you frightened at Mr. Hill? Hear me, I'll try."

"Is there a heart that never loved?
Or felt soft woman's sighs."

The old man puffed and blowed through the entire song, much to his own satisfaction.

"There, Mr. Hill, what do you think of that?"

"It is very well, sir, but it is not exactly as I have been in the habit of hearing it."

"Indeed! then, Mr. Hill, I wish you would let me hear your way."

"Mr. Hill then commenced,

"Is there a heart that never loved?"

and gave it, of course, correctly.

"Well, well, that is all very well, and very nice, I dare say, but I think I can do that song pretty well for a bass voice; but, lord! it's all a matter of taste; some would like yours and some mine. Mr. Hill, won't you tell sister one of your funny stories?"

"Oh do! he, he, he!" sniggered the maiden. "Oh, do!"

Mr. Hill looked her earnestly in the face and began:

"Did you ever hear of Deb Hawkins?"

"No, sir, he, he, he!" said the old lady, unconscious that Mr. Hill had commenced a story. "No, sir, I never heard of her in all my life."

"She is a shocking nice gal. Shouldn't wonder if she could make pumpkin pies good enough to make a fellow's mouth water. You see, I once courted her a little, just to see how it would feel."

"He, he, he!" tittered the old woman, her sympathies all excited.

"Says I to her one night, Deb, ain't you goin' to sit down on my knee nor nothin'. (The maiden lady put her handkerchief to her face.) Says Deb, putting her hand over her eyes, 'Oh, git eout, Joe,' so I tuck hold on her, and hauled her down. She squirmed round, but I held on of course, 'cause I know'd it was the natur of the critter."

"He, he, he! What a funny man you are, Mr. Hill."

"By and by, Deb got quieted down a spell, and took a kiss jest as easy."

"Oh, Mr. Hill, he, he, he!"

"Oh, she was an all fired nice gal, tew."

"Did she marry? he, he, he!" inquired the lady.

"I was goin' to say, she was an all fired nice gal to kiss, but phew! what a temper! It got so hot sometimes, it burnt a hole clean through her good manners."

So passed the evening at the house of the Alabamian. Mr. Hill was repaid for the misery of being obliged to listen to their musical efforts by being furnished with the material of an entertaining imitation, which was received by his audiences with great relish.

THE NERVOUS ARTIST.—THE GAMBLER RESCUED.

Mr. Hill's third visit to New Orleans was not only highly successful in a theatrical point of view, but replete with incidents of a character which Mr. Hill remembered with great satisfaction. During his passage down the Mississippi with Mr. Jarvis, an artist from Louisville, they became so attached to each other, that on their arrival in New Orleans, they engaged rooms in company. The Crescent City, at that time, bore quite a different reputation from that which it enjoys at present. Persons were frequently knocked down, and robbed in the streets, and mysterious assassination added its horrors to scenes of brawl and rowdyism. Mr. Jarvis was a man of an exceedingly nervous temperament, and timid to a degree. He was tremblingly alive to the danger which, as he supposed, beset the stranger at every turn in New Orleans, and always went armed to the teeth, although it is very doubtful if he could have mustered up sufficient nerve to use his weapons, had their use been needed. Besides Bowie knives, pistols, and other playthings of this character, he had a dog, and although it was one of the smallest kind of pet poodles, it was quite large enough to suggest to the ready mind of Mr. Hill, a sort of placebo to his friend's sense of danger. He very seriousl printed a placard containing the following ominous hint—"Take care of the Dog," which he posted up on the outside of their room door. The experiment succeeded to admiration, having only one little drawback, for it scared away friends, as well as less welcome intruders; for, of course, neither friend nor foe could tell from instinct, the size and ferocity of the animal of whom they were notified to beware. Things went on very smoothly, and Mr. Jarvis' throat was still uncut, and his wallet, safe with its contents, whatever they might have been, when, in the dead hour of the night, when all the world and his wife were fast asleep, Mr. Jarvis was awakened by heavy groans, which seemed to come from above, below, and all around him. Trembling with fear and agitation, he called upon his friend Hill, in the meantime taking his pistols from under his pillow, "Hill! Hill!" cried Jarvis—"for the love of heaven, wake up, or we shall be murdered in our beds!"

"What's the matter?" asked Mr. H.

"Matter! matter enough! I thought we should not get out of this infernal city without being robbed or murdered."

Mr. Hill scarcely comprehending what was the matter, nevertheless got out of bed; the valiant artist did the same, and handing a Bowie knife to Mr. Hill, courageously led the way to the top of the landing, with the fierce determination of quietly settling the hash of the supposed intruder.

"Stop! stop!" said Mr. Hill, "not so fast; if my ears do not deceive me, the groans proceed from that room down stairs, and are the cries of some person in distress."

"Nonsense," said Jarvis, "that's a mere ruse, and if we are not careful, we shall both be murdered."

"I am so convinced," replied Mr. Hill, "of the reality of my own suspicions, that I am determined to go to the room and ascertain the truth."

"Don't be rash," urged Jarvis, "they certainly will have your life if you go. Let us shoot them down."

Heedless of the caution, Mr. Hill hurried down stairs, leaving his friend Jarvis at the head of the steps shivering with cold and fear, with nothing on but his shirt, and a pair of large pistols in his hands. Mr. Hill soon reached the chamber from whence the groans proceeded. Sans ceremony, he opened the door and went in, and there, instead of encountering thieves and assassins, he found a poor woman suffering a maternal agony, without friends or attendance. He returned, with the view of sending Mr. Jarvis for assistance, whom he found still at his post, his pistols pointing down the stairs.

"Remove your pistols, Jarvis; don't fire at me; I'm not going to harm you."

"Well, well," said Jarvis, "have you found the villains? Where are they? Blow their brains out."

"You are quite mistaken," said Mr. Hill; "it is a poor woman sick and in need of immediate relief. Go to the landlady, and tell her to prepare some nourishment, and hasten to the servants' room. Then you retire to your room, and I will attend to the sufferer until she gets relief."

It is hardly necessary to say that it was fortunate for the poor woman that Mr. Hill knew of her distress, for it was not in his nature to leave anything undone which could contribute to her comfort. Twelve months after this event, Mr. Hill again visited New Orleans. He was walking down the street one day, arm-in-arm with a gentleman, when he saw a decently dressed Irishman and his wife hastening towards him.

"Oh! sure, Mr. Hill," said the woman, "and it's mesilf that's glad to see you; and isn't this a beautiful child?"

"Not a doubt about it, my good woman; but what have I to do with it?"

Mr. Hill had quite forgotten the circumstance I have related above.

"Is it what you have got to do wid it?" said the woman—"sure it would not have been here, and the image of his father, if you hadn't had something to do wid it."

Mr. Hill began to feel uncomfortable, for he found his friend giving him some significant digs in the ribs.

"My dear woman," said Mr. H.—"you must take me for somebody else."

"Divil a bit! D'ye think I'd ever forget the face of you? Can I ever forget when you found me alone, and got nurses and doctors to wait upon me, when I hadn't a friend in the wide world. Mistake you for somebody else! I'd never forget you till I die."

The circumstances of the case were recalled to Mr. Hill's mind, and putting a little present into the child's tiny fist, wished the grateful couple farewell. I don't know how he managed to satisfy his friend's mind, but this I know, his own was free from anything but a pleasant recollection of a circumstance which enabled him to render a kind service to a fellow-creature in distress.

On Mr. Hill's first visit to New-Orleans, he formed an intimacy with a Mr. S——, whom he found a gay-hearted, happy, and intelligent companion. On his third visit he was grieved to find, that the friend he had left so buoyant and gay, was bowed down with some inward sorrow. Instead of, as formerly, seeking the society of Mr. H., he avoided it. Mr. Hill was distressed at this, for he knew of no circumstance—having a sincere regard for his friend—which would justify this distant coolness on the part of Mr. S——. He resolved to fathom the mystery. From some little things he had observed, he formed a suspicion of the cause of his friend's depression, and he made up his mind, the first moment he was disengaged, to inquire further into the matter. On one of his off nights, he called at the residence of his friend, but he was told by the black boy, that "Massa was not at home, but that Missus was, and would be berry glad to see him." Mr. Hill, without hesitation, followed the servant to the drawing-room; he there found Mrs. S—— in tears. Mr. H., taking the privilege of an old friend, asked her the cause of her sadness.

"Oh! Mr. Hill," she replied, "I am very unhappy; I have not seen Charles since yesterday morning. He now frequently leaves me days together, and seems so altered, that I am almost heart-broken."

"Nay, nay, my dear madam," said Mr. Hill, "do not despond; it may be nothing but a temporary estrangement; some passing excitement which keeps him away. Be of good heart, all will yet be right. I made up my mind to discover the cause of his avoidance of me, and now that he is estranged from you and his home, I have a double incentive to use every exertion to reclaim the truant."

With such blessings as a young, affectionate and confiding, but neglected wife, alone could call down upon one promising to restore all she held dear in life, Mr. Hill departed to put his plans in execution.

In a remote corner of the city of New-Orleans, was situated one of those fashionable dens of vice, where men staked honor, virtue, and fortune, on the turning of a die; where swindlers were educated, and assassins learned their trade. It was midnight; and at the faro-table stood one conspicuous from the rest, whose face wore an expression of unspeakable anguish. His last counter was in his hand, and thoughts of home, of wife and children, came crowding upon his distracted brain; but alas! instead of staying his progress, the ruin he had brought upon his family, but urged him on. Fortune might change, and if once redeemed, he would forswear for ever the maddening game. Just as he was putting down his last stake, a stranger enveloped in a large cloak, his face almost hidden with a pair of large, black whiskers, and his head covered with a fur cap of most uncouth appearance, rushed into the room. He looked more like a *demon* than a human being, and the effect of his appearance not only suspended the games, but seemed to paralyze the players, for "conscience makes cowards of us all." In the confusion which followed this sudden intrusion, of they knew not whom, the lights were put out. Mr. S——, for it was he who stood so conspicuously at the faro-table, found himself grasped by the arm, and led forcibly away. He was too much dismayed by the suddenness of the whole affair to offer resistance, and he went whither he was led. When he was in the street, the lamp disclosed to him that he was in the hands of the stranger whose sudden appearance had produced so much commotion in the gambling-house. It was but the work of a moment for the stranger to take the whiskers from his face, and reveal to the astonished gamester the face of his friend, Mr. Hill.

"Now, sir," said Mr. Hill, sternly, "I hope you have had

enough of that infernal place, and will never return to it again."

Overwhelmed with shame and oonfusion, it was some time before S—— could reply.

"Oh, God !" said he at length, "what shall I do ? I have lost every cent I had in the world. I never can look upon my wife again."

"You must see your wife, and that without delay, if you wish me to stand by you in this hour of distress. But come—let us hasten on, or we may be overtaken by some of your associates, and I fancy, from the slight glimpse I had of them, neither of us would be very safe in their hands. Before we meet your wife, tell me, Charles, what you intend to do ; will you, if I refund the money, you have lost to-night, promise on your honor, never to set foot in a gambling-house again ?"

"I will, George, my more than brother," replied S——, overcome by the kindness which offered redemption. "I will do all that man can do, not only to recover your confidence but to deserve it."

"Enough ; I believe you," said Mr. Hill. "Now I have a little explanation to make. A day or two after my arrival in this city, I was persuaded by a friend to visit the same hell which you have just left. As I went in, I thought I saw your figure retreating from the room. I considered the matter well, and the more I thought of it, the stronger became the impression that it was you whom I saw. This gave me the key to your mysterious avoidance of me, and I determined to seek you there: the result you know. But to return to my own visit. You know the arts they employ to gain the confidence of the unsuspecting, and how frequently they will permit the man who is known to have means, to win. They tried this decoy upon me, and when I left the room that evening, I was the winner of three hundred dollars. I purposed to give this amount to some charitable institution—it is yours, Charles, and as much more is at your service as you staked at 'that desperate game, last evening."

S—— was too much overcome to speak his thanks. He had in some measure conquered his emotion by the time he reached home. They found Mrs. S—— sitting up, watching the return of her truant husband. Mr. Hill did not give time for reproaches, but pushing Mr. S—— into the arms of his wife, said, "There, madam, not a word, there will be no more absence from home—all is right. Now, good night—God bless you."

Mr. S—— is now the father of three blooming children, and one of the most prosperous merchants of New-Orleans.

A MEETING UPON THE SUBJECT OF THE PUBLIC PRESS.

I DO not know, whether or not, the characters which figure below, at a meeting held for the Quixotic purpose of putting down the Press, are the same who recently met in New-York, to devise means of stopping the issue of Sunday papers, but if they are not, they might readily be mistaken for them, only the error would involve a degree of flattery which I do not think the latter deserve. Mr. Hill attended the meeting, of which the following is his faithful report. Mr. Obadiah Sleek, who presided on this occasion, said :

" Brethren, we have met here for the purpose of suppressing the Press. There are many articles in the daily newspaper very injurious to the morals of the rising generation, particularly the young, and being impressed with that impression, I wish to express myself to you, and have it impressed on your minds in the most pressing manner."

The Chairman having delivered himself of this impressive speech, sat down. Brother Longjaw now addressed the meeting :

" I have heard the very eloquent and lengthy remarks of Mr. Sleek, and I must say I entirely coincide with his views. There are a great number of persons in the westerly diggins of our town, who coincide with him tew, and they told me to tell you that they entirely coincided with you in your views, let them be what they might."

Oziah Slimbrain, he spoke:

"Mr. Cheerman, I don't think as how I ought to say anything, 'cause I've got nothing to say; but if all men who spoke at public meetings, didn't speak till they had something to say, speakers would be rather scarce. I goes in agin papers: what is the good of 'em to a man as can't read? I took hold of one once, but I got it wrong eend up. In my young days larning was dear, and I didn't go to school but one day in my life, and that was in the evening, and the master was not there, all of which convinces me papers should be put down. Our folks at hum would have all come to this meeting, but they've been busy making cherry rum, and they throwed the cherries out behind the barn, and Jedide and the hogs have been eating them, and we've got the darn'dest lot of corned pork you ever did see. Jedide said it wasn't eating the cherries, but swallowing the stones, that corned the hogs. Aunt Jerusha was a coming to this meeting, but she's got the measles, and she was afraid of making a breaking out in the meeting, but I made made up my mind I'd come myself, so I hitched the old mare up to the waggon, but she came along so tarnal slow, that I licked her, and then she slewed the old waggon right up agin the fence all to smash. I tied the tarnal old critter up with her blind eye to the road, so that she'll think she's bang up agin the fence, and stay there just as quiet. I don't care now, however, for I have got here a darned sight quicker than I should if I'd driv her. Now I've got here, I don't know what to say agin the papers, more than I think they should be put down. I see you are a putting down names; you may put down all our family—Jedide, Jeruse, and the hogs, if you like—I don't care a darn."

Mr. Slam next rose to address the meeting. It is impossible to repeat the substance of this gentleman's remarks. He appeared to have got up in a passion. Every word he uttered was followed by a savage blow upon the table, and when he got very much excited, he would strike it a dozen times, speaking all the while, but the noise he made completely drowned his words. The following is as near a report as we can make in writing:

"Mr. Chairman, (bang!) I presume (bang! bang!)—yes, sir, I repeat it—(bang! bang!) sir, (bang!) certainly they should be put down—(bang! bang! bang!) that is what—(bang!) with these few remarks, I submit—(bang!) my resolution."

John Holdtight spoke next—

Mr. Ch—Ch—Chairman, I—I—I— el—abor under s—s—su—such di—di—di—difficulties in sp—sp—speaking, that I—I bul—bul—bul—ieve I sh—sh—shall say noth—noth—nothing about it."

A stranger got up—

"Mr. Chairman: John Hopper told me to say to you that he was very sorry he could not attend this meeting. John Hopper's horse not being shod, he could not attend this meeting. If it had been shod, John Hopper would have attended this meeting; but by reason of John Hopper's horse not being shod, he could not come. The man who shods John Hopper's horse being out on a drunken frolic, he could not get his horse shod, and consequently John Hopper's horse not being shod, he could not attend this meeting."

An effeminate voice from the back part of the meeting was then heard—

"Mr. Chairman: I don't feel altogether clean-handed. I have been a good deal lately in the habit of reading the papers, and I say, I don't feel altogether clean-handed. I have been in the habit of reading the *weeklies*, being more appropriate to a man like me of a *weakly* constitution. I have known some articles appearing therein, which ought to have been thrown out, and I don't feel altogether clean-handed."

The Chairman now spoke:

"I find my brethren, that my views have been completely carried out, and when I have stated what I am about to state, that I should mention that I mean to state this meeting is adjourned."

COUSIN GUSS.

"Well, how de dew? I'm right glad to see you, I swow. I rather guess I can say suthin' about the *Revolution* business, purty good varsion, tew, by jingo. My father, old Josh Addams, had his fist in it: any on you know him? Old Josh Addams, as well known as the Schuylkill water-works. He was born in Boston: he didn't die there, 'cause he died in Philadelphia. He used to wear an old genuine '76 coat, little cut down to suit the fashion, made it a razee. One might have known the old man a mile off. If it hadn't been for Cousin Guss, he'd have been livin to this ere day. You may see Guss in Chestnut street,—any of you know him?—dressed like a peacock, and got whiskers big enough to stuff a sofa bottom. He went down t'other day, to see the wild beasts in 5th street; jest as he was comin' away, he met a hull squad of little children a comin' in: when they saw Cousin Guss, if they didn't *squeal* like ten thousand *devils*. The old man says, what's the matter, young ones? Oh dear, papa, see, they've let one of the monkeys loose. Cousin Guss didn't show his face in Chestnut street for a week. Guss *telled* the old man he must have his coat cut again, and altered to the fashion; so he coaxed old Josh to let him take it down to his ——, as he called him, down in 3d street. Well, the good-natured old critter said he might: when he got it back, sich a lookin' thing as it was, you might have fallen down and worshipped it, without breaking the ten commandments. When we saw it, we all larfed; sister Jedide, she snickered right out. The old man looked at it for about a minute, didn't say a word, by jingo,—the tears rolled out of his eyes as big as hail-stones. He jest folded it up, put it under his pillow, laid himself down on the bed, and never got up again: it broke his heart: he died from a curtailed coat.

"The old man used to tell sich stories about the Revolution. I rather guess he could say a leetle more about that affair than most folks. 'Bout six years ago he went to Boston, when La Fayette was there; they gave a great dinner at Fanueil Hall. When the Mayor heard Old Josh Addams was in Boston, he sent him a regular built invitation. The old man went, and wore the '76 coat,—that is, before it was cut down, though. By-and-bye they called upon the old man for a *toast*. Up he got, and says he, 'Here's to the Heroes of the Revolution, who fought, bled, and died, for their country, of which I was one.' When old Josh said that, they all snickered right out.

"There's one story the old man used to tell about Boston, that was a real snorter: he always used to laugh afore he begun. He said, down on Long Wharf there was a queer little feller,—a cousin of his by the mother's side, —called Zedekiah Hales, who wasn't more than four foot high, and had a hump jest between his shoulders. A hull squad of British officers got round Zedekiah, in State street, and were laughing and poking all sorts of fun at him: he bore it, cause as how he couldn't help it; one of them, a regular built dandy captain, lifting up his glass, said to him, 'You horrid little deformed critter, what' that lump you've got on your shoulder?' Zedekiah turned round and looked at him for about a *minute,* and says he, 'it's *Bunker Hill,* you tarnal fool, you.'"

TWO BIRDS KILLED WITH ONE STONE.

Mr. Hill, on one of the occasions of his benefit, sent persons to every part of the City of Boston, to get all the cripples they could find, to call at the office of Dr. ——, —a young physician, at that time, having but a limited practice,—where they would receive aid and advice gratis. The doctor was not aware of what was going on, but he was very much astonished at the sudden increase of his practice: his office was besieged with the halt, the lame, and the blind. The doctor turned none away, and in a great many of the cases, had the satisfaction of doing a great deal of good. Public notice was shortly attracted to the office of this physician, and he soon enjoyed a large and lucrative practice. Many of the patients acted for Mr. Hill's benefit, representing the army of Bombastes, and such an army of real deformities was certainly never seen on any stage before.

THE TWO FAT SALS.

If every man were to relate the little romances of love in which he becomes involved, at some time or other of his life, novelists and farce-writers would be supplied with plots and incidents enough to supply publishers and managers with a continual run of novelties for all times. In the story of the "Two fat Sals," which Mr. Hill used to relate with such inimitable humor, is recorded the experience of one man only, but it affords a very useful lesson on the evils of a mind divided in the matter of love, and another illustrious example of the truth of the aphorism, that "the course of true love never did run smooth."

"There was two Sals livin' in our town, Sal Stebbins and Sal Babit,—real corn-fed gals, I swow. Sal Stebbins would lift a barrel of cider out of the eend of a cart as quick as any other feller, and drink it tew. Sal Babit, she was so fat, she'd roll one way jest as easy as t'other, and if anything, a little *easier*. Well, there was a corn-husking, and I went along with Sal Stebbins: there was all the gals and boys settin' reound, and I got sot down so near Sal Babit, that I'll be darned if I didn't kiss her afore I know'd what I was abeout. Sal Stebbins, she blushed: the blood rushed right up into her hair: she was the best *red* critter I ever did see. I thought it was all up with me, and sure enough it was, for when I asked her if she would go hum with me, she said 'no; you needn't trouble yourself nothin' 'tall 'beout it.' 'Well, if you're mind to get spunky, I guess I can git a gal that will let me see her hum. Sal Babit, shall I go hum with you?' 'Well,' says she, 'I don't mind if you dew.' Arter that, Sal Stebbins married a feller in our town, by the name of *Post*,—blind in one eye, and deaf in one ear,—jest to spite me, nothin' else: so I thought if she was a mind to take a feller that couldn't see or hear any tew well, I'd better let her slide: so I went away from hum, and was gone about three—four—five years?—yes, jest about five years, 'cause I know when I got back she had four little *Posts*. I went to see how she got along. She asked me to come in and set down; so I tuck a cheer and squatted: then she tuck another cheer and squatted; and we both squatted there together. Her young ones was all runnin' reound on the floor: she pinted to them, and said, in a sort of bragging way, 'You see them, don't you?' 'Yes,' says I, squintin' up one eye, 'I see, they're all jest like their daddy, blind in one eye.' She was bilin' dumplings at the time, and as soon as she see me shut up one eye, she out with a hot dumplin', and let me have it in t'other, which made me shut it up a darn'd sight quicker than I ever did afore, and I haint been in love since that time."

A LEARNED SOCIETY.

New England is studded with learned societies. The people of the Eastern States seem to be as curious in matters of science as they are in prying into each other's affairs. Boston alone, every year, brings out more new isms and ologies, than all the other cities in the Union put together. I most sincerely believe, that if some vast scientific discovery were to be made to-day among some newly found people, whose language was different from anything ever thought of or conceived before, that in a week, some Yankee or other would advertise a lecture upon the subject, and maybe deliver it in the new tongue. The following report of a Learned Society, Mr. Hill attended in Clamtown, I give as he used to relate it.

YANKEE CABALA.

"Old Samuel Winston, Esq., a member of our Historical Society in Clamtown, was considered a 'notionate critter,' and one of his notions was *Cabala*. He considered himself learned upon the subject. There were belonging to the same society, a number of the sons of one Jacob Bigelow. Said Jacob, had twelve children, and these young ones were continually plaguing old Sammy to give a lecture before the society, on Cabalistic Science, or show them what it was like. He at length consented, and here is a copy of the result of his labor. This diagram was unrolled before the society, and the Bigelows in particular.—

"Cabalistic Science is a cute arrangement of picters, figures and letters, so as tew mean suthin' and here is an example of how sich arrangements due read. (*Points to* 1.)

"In course nobody kin take offence at what kin be made eout of figures and letters, for you kin jist make eout on 'em what you've a mind tew. None ony ou see offence in this? (*Diagram.*)

All answered "No," and the Bigelows louder than the rest.

"Well then, put in your mind that this is the key tew the hull science, and you kin here trace it. (*Counts Diagram, One.*)

A member interrupted him with—

"Wouldn't you like to have a large door key, Squire Winston, it might be better to pint the subject eout."

WINSTON,—"You better be quiet. I b'lieve you don't know Cabala, I b'lieve."

ANOTHER MEMBER.—"Squire, is Cabala any derivation from gabble, tew keep up a talkin'?"

WINSTON.—"You are a fool too, you are, I b'lieve. Shut up your talkin'."

2d MEMBER.—"Well, dew go on with that key. Patience, *m-a-s-sy*, you will be so long, and so tigious, that I shouldn't be a mite surprised, if your key got me locked eout tew home."

WINSTON.—"The key! that is this key."

3d Member.—"Well, dew strike that *key,* will you? you'll never git through it. I never did see anything like the prosyness of that critter; dew go on."

Winston.—"I'll thank you, Mr. President, to keep this society a little quieter; it is gittin tew be a parfect bedlam of ignorance, I b'lieve."

3d Member.—"Dew you mean to say, that you are the key stun of the whole society yourself."

Winston.—(*Picking up a specimen.*) "I mean that I will throw a stun at your head, if you don't lock up your tongue."

He proceeds,—

"Take this key, (*points to key,*) and place it on this, and you kin spell eout *Jacob Bigelow.* Now read down this list, (*points to names,*) and you have the names of his sons—critters, at whose persuasion I have gin this lecture. Here you have a picter, or set of picters, which in course mean suthin', and thus they read. (*Names the pictures.*)

"Well, put this key on them picters, and you can spell by the first letters with this key, Jacob Bigelow, agin,—old Jacob's most sensible expressions on any occasion, was '*git eout*' or '*dew tell,*' and by applying the key, here you have 'em. Examine the same letters which say this, and you see they are the initial letters of the whole family. These picters not only spell the old man's name, but they exhibit the propensities of his children. (*Names in Diagram* 6.)

"The Bigelow family wanted tew larn Cabalistic science; here is a specimen, heow do they like it?"

This is what old Mr. Winston termed a *Yan-key* way of shutting the hull Bigelow family up. Here was a row in which all joined. The mystic Cabala had been deciphered, and the Bigelows struck into a high key. Winston, was standing with his divining rod in his hand on a bench, and every now and then, you could hear him shout in a roaring key—

WINSTON.—"It is a correct key, and you may like it or not, I b'lieve."

The Landlady who owned the house, lived in one end, and rented the apartments to the Society, with key in hand, visited the room, when she broke into a shrill key—(She had rented the house to catch a beau from the Society.)

LANDLADY.—"Oh, gracious! dew you mean tew ruin a widow, jist in her prime, who only owns this house, and six others in the town jist like it, and has a new set of china and furnitur, and no incumbrances; I say, dew this Society of gentlemen, among whom I see a few widder acquaintances, and some bachelors, young and old, who ought to have been settled down in life long ago; dew you, by the combined power of your healthy voices, by shoutin' in this eoutrageous key of voice, both young and old on you, married and unmarried, not forgettin' the widowers, I say, dew you all want tew, in this manner, break the peace and quietness of a poor widow, by breakin' on her up. Ef you don't all jist clear out, I'll lock every one on you in the house till mornin'."

The Landlady shook her *key* at the Society, and there was a *Yan-key* meaning in it, which broke up the historical *Cabal*, who, on this occasion had become so *Cabalistic.*

AN ADVENTURE ON HORSEBACK.

On one of Mr. Hill's visits to New Orleans, he rode out on horseback with a friend of his, and, as they were passing the St. Charles Hotel, his companion said,

"Hill, I dare you to ride up those steps;"—meaning those which led to the large reading-room attached to that magnificent Hotel.

"You dare me, do you?" said Mr. Hill.

"Yes; but if you will do it, I will forfeit this fifty dollars."

"I don't want your money, but here goes."

He put spurs to his horse, and quick as a flash was up the steps and into the reading-room. It was filled with gentlemen engaged in a quiet perusal of the papers, but such scampering and confusion which followed the appearance of the gentleman on horseback, can be better imagined than described. They scattered in all directions, while the rider, nothing daunted, walked his horse leisurely round the room, making a sort of genteel waltz among the chairs and tables, When they found who it was that had thus intruded his horsemanship upon their especial notice, they all enjoyed the joke, with the exception of one old gentleman, who went to the bar and demanded his bill, declaring he would not remain a moment in a house where such doings were allowed. Mr. Hill frequently met the irrate old gentleman in the street, but he always gave Mr. H. a wide berth. He seemed fearful that if he went too near Mr. Hill, a horse would spring up under the legs of the latter gentleman, and trample him to death. This was, I believe, the first and only time Mr. H. performed on horseback.

A ROMANCE OF THE CITY.

After his return from the West, he appeared in Boston, and immediately afterward in Philadelphia. During his sojourn in the City of Brotherly Love, he met Mr. G., an old associate and confidant of his, who was about to be married. Mr. G., on meeting his friend Hill, expressed an anxious desire that he should go with him to the house of his intended, and see the lady to whom he was about to submit his happiness and fortune. Mr. Hill, of course, readily consented, for it was not in his nature to refuse the performance of an act which would even oblige a stranger, still less an old and much esteemed friend. Mr. G. was anxious to have Mr. Hill's opinion of the lady of his choice, little doubting, perhaps, but that it would be a flattering confirmation of his own judgment. In this, however, he was mistaken. Mr. Hill did not see the lady, as did his friend, with the eyes of love, and he saw in the gay, affected, and coquettish manner of Miss R., a frivolity of mind and gaiety of disposition which would be the rock upon which the happiness of his friend would surely be wrecked. Mr. Hill would gladly have avoided the giving an opinion upon the subject, for he knew full well the little weight an adverse judgment has with a man in love; but his friend was not to be driven from his purpose, and insisted upon

Mr. Hill giving a truthful account of the impression on his mind in relation to the lady. Thus urged, Mr. Hill remarked:

"My dear fellow, your intended is pretty, sings well, and has a graceful manner, but she is vain, and too fond of admiration to rest satisfied with the regard of you alone."

"But I think she loves me sincerely?"

"Yes; perhaps as well as she is capable of loving; but I could not help thinking,—for I watched her closely all the evening,—that you have touched her vanity and not her heart. You occupy a fine position in society, possessing both wealth and reputation, and if I do her not great injustice, she looks upon you rather as the means of her enjoyment, than the source of her happiness. You insist upon my opinion, and I give it without any scruples of delicacy. She appears to me utterly destitute of those solid qualities calculated to make your fireside happy; and I would beg you, if you can with honor, to withdraw from your engagement, for I can see nothing in its fulfilment but disappointment and misery."

As my readers have, probably, already anticipated, the advice, though sought, was not taken, and in a very short time after this conversation his friend was married. Mr. Hill went to England soon after this, and did not see Mr. G. again, until the year 1840. Twenty years seemed to have laid their burden of cares upon him. He was no longer the pleasant and jovial companion Mr. Hill had known him, but a care-worn, heart-broken man. His wife, on the contrary, appeared gayer than ever. Home had no attractions for her, and the society of her husband was the last she sought. Mr. Hill's worst anticipations had been more than realized. A separation eventually took place: Mr. G. went to Europe, and his wretched wife abandoned herself to a life of profligacy and shame. I may as well relate, here, the sequel of this story, although the scene took place years afterwards.

In the year 1846, Mr. Hill resided in Fourth street, near Union Square, New York. Whilst residing here, he practised as a dentist, and as all who follow this profession assume the title of Doctor, he was not unfrequently called upon to officiate in that capacity. He was awakened from his sleep, one night, by a loud ringing of the bell. He got up, put on his wrapper, and went to the door.

"Oh, docther, dear, won't you come and see a poor sick creature who is dangerous, and is lying in a room, forenenst the one my wife and children live in."

"My friend, there is a doctor lives next door; call upon him, and I've no doubt he will readily go with you."

"I've done that same, and he is not at home. Oh, what will I do; and there's no other docther near."

"Oh, if that's the case," said Mr. Hill, "and I can be of any use, I'll go with you."

"Long life to you for that same."

Mr. Hill accompanied the man to a wretched tenement, above Fourteenth street. He went into the room of the sick woman, and who should he recognize in the miserable object before him, but the once gay and fashionable Mrs. G., the wife of his old friend. Feeble as she was, after a while she recognized Mr. Hill, and oh, what words of bitter anguish and repentance escaped her parched lips. Now, when sickness and poverty had worn off the gilding which pleasure employs to hide its unsubstantial nature, the affections she had lost, the home she had made desolate, the love she had deceived, the hopes she had betrayed, came crowding upon her heart and mind to add the poignancy of their bitter thoughts to the agony of a bodily dissolution. Mr. Hill did and said all that he could to soothe and comfort her, but who can administer to a mind diseased ? Only he who could recall to the dying wretch the golden opportunities she had lost ; who could bring back youth and health,— and no such patient spirit dwells on earth. The pillow may be smoothed, the sharp pain blunted, the fever which burns may be relieved ; but the mind diseased, the heart betrayed, must look to higher than human power. To this Mr. Hill directed the feelings of the dying woman, and he had the consolation of knowing, that, before she died, which was in a few days after this interview, she became sober and resigned

MISPLACED AFFECTION.

At lovers' vows they say Jove laughs, but, by Jove, they ought sometimes to make him weep, if he were a respectable and gentlemanly man, as he ought to be, from age and position. If he could but take his place in some of our modern courts of justice, and listen to the details of lovers' perjuries, as displayed in *crim. con.* suits, now and then, or in the more romantic cases of "Breaches of Promise," I fancy the "Ancient" would laugh on the other side of his mouth.

The following story of misplaced affection, also, has its suggestions of sorrow and regret, at which it would be very naughty in Jove even to smile, much less laugh.

"Mr. D——, a merchant of the city of New York, was associated also with a mercantile house in Boston, the business transactions of which frequently required his presence in the latter city. He was accustomed to spend his evenings on such occasions, at the residence of his partner. On one of these visits, he met Miss S——, an extremely pretty and interesting, but, as the sequel will show, a very weak girl. Mr. D—— was a man of intelligence, agreeable in manners, and of prepossessing appearance. He could talk fluently and intelligibly of the ordinary and extraordinary topics of the day, and had sufficient tact not to venture upon subjects which required more thought than a man constantly busied with cottons and calicoes can give to anything which does not appear beside the money article or price-current of a daily paper. He husbanded his stock of knowledge very adroitly, and placing his best goods in the shop window of his mind, managed to attract the attention of such superficial folks as Miss S——. She conceived for Mr. D—— a romantic attachment, which she had not the strength of mind or principle to resist, or even the cunning to conceal. In a moment of thoughtless enthusiasm, she confessed to him how dear he had become to her, and how impossible it was for her to live without him. He, instead of being startled with the confession of a guilty love like this, and checking, at once, a passion which could not but result in certain misery to all concerned, allowed his vanity to get the mastery of his judgment, yielded to the unholy influence which was fast spreading around him. He was a married man, and, excepting this circumstance, loved his wife devotedly. Like many others, feeling his heart secure, he imagined he could throw aside the parasitic feeling which but clung, as he thought, only upon the outside of his affections, whenever he thought proper. Dangerous infatuation! fatal error! The ivy clings not more tenaciously to the oak, than do the spreading tendrils, which shoot from a corrupted heart around the principles of those who carelessly encourage their creeping insidiousness. Mr. D——, by not at once quenching the guilty flame which was burning in the bosom of Miss S——, committed a grievous fault, which, but for the interposition of a friend in time, might have rendered his own fireside a domestic ruin, and brought the gray hairs of an aged parent with sorrow to the grave.

Mr. Hill, who was acquainted with all the parties, was playing an engagement in Boston, when the mother of Miss S—— came to him, and begged his advice and assistance. She informed him, that her erring daughter had left her home and followed Mr. D—— to New York, and begged him, as he was about to leave for that city, to use his influence in urging her truant child to return. Mr. Hill readily promised to exert himself to that effect. He called on Miss S—— on his arrival in New York. Mr. Hill, not harshly, but earnestly pictured to her the certain misery she was bringing upon herself and all connected with her, by pursuing the course she seemed to have marked out for herself. He then informed her, that her mother had commissioned him to conduct her back to Boston, but to this she would not listen. "What is your object," said Mr. Hill, "in remaining in the city?" She made no reply, and Mr. H. told her somewhat impatiently, that he knew why she would not leave, "And, madam," said he, "I can see nothing but ruin to yourself and to the man you pretend to love, in a persistence in this wretched conduct. What, if you take your lover from the bosom of the woman he has sworn to love; can you expect a moment's happiness? can you rely upon the feelings of a man who can so easily be decoyed away; but no, you will not be a party to such a thing. You have been blinded by passion. I will now leave you, and in the afternoon, having given you till that time for reflection, I will again call to learn your decision."

Mr. H. saw that the most prompt measures must be employed to wake up the infatuated girl to a proper sense of her degrading position, and after giving the subject due consideration, he decided upon calling on Mrs. D——, the wife, and informing her of the affair as it then stood. It was a painful task, but he thought it the most likely way to startle Mr. D—— to a sense of duty, and he resolved to do it. He was surprised, in calling upon Mrs. D——, to discover that she knew all about it, and had in her possession a letter from Miss S——, to Mr. D——. At Mr. Hill's request, Mrs. D—— called upon Miss S——. When Mrs. D—— introduced herself and showed the deluded girl the letter, the latter was ready to sink with mortification and shame. Not a loophole was left for her escape; no excuse could be offered, for in her own handwriting were the damning proofs of the injury she was inflicting upon the innocent wife, who stood before her. No harsh reproaches escaped the lips of the injured wife: no useless recriminations to call a retort from the guilty girl; but Mrs. D——, with the noble spirit of Him who said to the adultress, "go thou, and sin no more," kindly pointed out the error of her way, and urged her, ere it were too late, to fly to her home, and to her distracted mother. Overcome by the dignity of the woman, whose happiness she had so nearly destroyed, she burst into tears, and declared she would never see Mr. D—— again. "Pardon and forgive me," said she, "he told me you were cold to him, that you did not care for him, and I was bewildered. He has basely traduced the noblest of women, and the best of wives: take back his miniature he gave me. Oh, that I had never seen him." Mrs. D—— encouraged her in her determination, and parted from her in kindness and charity. Mr. Hill called in the afternoon and was pleased to find Miss S—— dressed, and ready for a speedy departure. Mr. H.

did not leave her till he saw her safe on the Boston steamer, on her way to her friends and home. Years have passed since these circumstances transpired, and I have reason to know that the promise she gave in a moment of poignant sorrow and shame was faithfully kept during years of changing prosperity and fortune.

THREE CHANCES FOR A WIFE.

WHEN a man has three chances for a wife, it is, indeed, a hard mischance if he should fail. The following is one of those cases, which might have occurred down east, but I am rather doubtful if a similar event was ever known in any other part of the world. But let me give the experience of the gentleman, who had three chances, in his own language:

"I once courted a gal by the name of Deb Hawkins. I made it up to get married. Well, while we was going up to the deacon's, I stepped my foot into a mud puddle, and spattered the mud all over Deb Hawkins' new gown, made out of her grandmother's old chintz petticoat. Well, when we got to the deacon's, he asked Deb if she would take me for her lawful wedded husband? 'No,' says she, 'I shan't do no such thing.' 'What on airth is the reason?' says I. 'Why,' says she, 'I've taken a mislikin' to you.' Well, it was all up with me then, but I give her a string of beads, a few kisses, some other notions, and made it all up with her; so we went up to the deacon's a second time. I was determined to come up to her this time, so when the deacon asked me if I would take her for my lawfully wedded wife, says I, 'No, I shan't do no such thing.' 'Why,' says Deb. 'what on airth is the matter?' 'Why,' says I,

'I have taken a mislikin' to you now.' Well, there it was all up again, but I gave her a new apron, and a few other little trinkets, and we went up again to get married. We expected then we would be tied so fast that all nature couldn't separate us, and when we asked the deacon if he wouldn't marry us, he said 'No, I shan't dew any sich thing.' 'Why, what on airth is the reason?' says we. 'Why,' says he, 'I've taken a mislikin' to both on you.' Deb burst out cryin', the deacon burst out scolding, and I burst out laughing, and sich a set of reg'lar busters you never did see."

SURGICAL AMBITION.—THE SPIRIT WILLING BUT THE FLESH WEAK.

Mr. Hill had a passion for everything appertaining to surgery, but he had in his composition too much of the milk of human kindness to stand with a bold front to witness the suffering consequent upon surgical operations. He often expressed his appreciation of excellence in the art, and frequently desired an opportunity to be present in the hospital when some great operation was to be performed. One of his friends rallied him upon his want of courage, and to test it, offered to accompany him to the hospital on the next operating day. Mr. Hill accepted the invitation. On the day on which Mr. Hill was introduced, the operating theatre was crowded, as the celebrated Dr. Warren was going to perform one of those bold operations for which he is so famous. Hill bore the preparatory steps with considerable composure; but when the patient was seated in the chair, in which he was to undergo the agony of a severe and tedious operation, his sympathies were painfully excited, and his courage was evidently like Bob Acres, in the Rivals, about to make its exit by way of his fingers. The accomplished surgeon took his scalpel and made the first incision. Hill's face was pale as marble: he held his fingers to his ears that the groans of the tortured patient might not be heard, but all was of no avail, and he left the theatre with as much haste as possible, and sauntered about the wards of the hospital until all was over.

In one of the beds lay a patient, who, a short time previously, had lost a leg by amputation. The patient knew Mr. Hill, and spoke to him. Mr. Hill did his best to get up a little courage, and made a dismal effort to assume a professional indifference, but the sick man saw, thought, and said, with a serio-comic air, "Ah, Mr. Hill, you won't do for a doctor. This is a horrid place for a Christian to be in. My leg is gone, but I don't care for that. My wife and children"—and here the sick man paused. Hill's hand had been fumbling in his pocket, and at last he drew out an eagle, and threw it to the sick man. "There, send that to your wife, and if she don't want to use it, keep it to buy yourself a wooden leg when you get well." Mr. Hill took a hurried departure from the hospital; and although he never lost a keen sensibility to the suffering of his fellow-creatures, his love of the surgical profession prevailed sufficiently to enable him to witness operations afterwards with some fortitude.

LOVERS' QUARRELS.—RECONCILIATION.

On Mr. Hill's first visit to London, he was introduced to the family of Mr. T——, of ——, near Regent's Park. He had the faculty, in an eminent degree, of making those with whom he came in contact, love him. There was a frank, hearty manner about him which abhorred concealments, and I have been surprised in reading over some of the papers in my possession to see with what readiness he obtained the confidence of others. The family of Mr. T——, consisting of his wife and three daughters, entertained the highest regard for Mr. Hill, and as will be seen by the sequel, one member of the family made him a sort of father confessor, in a very delicate affair; this was the eldest daughter. Mr. Hill had observed that, during his last visit to the family, this young lady had lost all her vivacity, and seemed depressed and melancholy. She had been playing at the piano, accompanied by Mr. Hill with his flute, when she suddenly gave up playing, and retired to the sofa. It so happened, there was no one in the room beside themselves. Mr. Hill, in his usual kind manner, inquired the cause of her sadness. "Oh, not much!" she replied, "my health has not been as well as usual, lately." "Excuse me, my dear Miss T——, but I think there is something more. If you have any cause of unhappiness confide your sorrow to me, and if I cannot remove the cause of your depression, the sympathy of a friend will, perhaps, alleviate it: come now." She was silent for a moment, and looking at Mr. Hill through her tears, said "You are right, Mr. Hill, I am truly miserable, and I dare not let my mother or sisters know the cause. I have been for some months partially engaged to Mr. P———, but I felt that he did not love me with that devotion that I wished, and I determined to try the strength of his attachment. About three weeks ago we were all at a party, and I was introduced to a young man, who during the evening paid me a great deal of attention, which I encouraged—in fact we appeared devoted to each other. I occasionally glanced towards him whom I truly loved, to see the effect my conduct produced. I saw that he was hurt, and yet I persisted in my unfeeling course. At length he was missing from the room. At first I thought nothing of his absence, but when I found he did not return, my heart sank within me, and I ordered the carriage and went home. The next day I received a letter from him, in which he said that he had witnessed, with unspeakable anguish, my conduct of the evening before, and that he should now take leave of me forever, hoping that now I had found one better suited to my tastes and inclination, and should be happy. He released me from all engagements. He confessed that he loved me." "I see," said Mr. Hill, "you have acted unkindly; but tell me, if your lover could be convinced of the true state of the case, and could be restored to you, would you venture to trifle with his feelings so again?" "Never!" she earnestly replied. "Well, then, leave the matter to me; I know him well; and will let him understand how you feel, without compromising your delicacy in the least." Mr. Hill was then preparing to visit Paris, whither Mr. P—— had fled, under the disappointments he had experienced. One of the first things Mr. Hill did, on reaching Paris, was to find out Mr. P——. He had not his address, but he ransacked all the public places in the hope of meeting the truant, but with no success, for some time. At length, whilst taking some refreshments in a celebrated café, who should come in but the melancholy lover. He was delighted at seeing Mr. Hill, for he knew he should hear news from home, and especially of her to whom his heart was still devoted, despite her coquetry. Mr. Hill found no difficulty in approaching the subject, for it was one, of all others, Mr. P—— was most interested in. When the true state of the case was made known, he was for starting back to England by the first conveyance, but Mr. Hill restrained the impatient lover, and made him promise to stay until the next day, which he did. Paris had now lost all attractions for him, and not one moment longer than that would he be detained.

On Mr. Hill's return to England, he found the young lady he left so melancholy and depressed, the gayest of the gay. Her color had come back to her cheeks, and when he suddenly went into the room where she and her lover were seated, she flew to receive him, and—shall I say it—kissed him. The lover was by, and had sense enough to attribute this kiss of gratitude to the right source. They were married in a few months after, and are now as happy a couple as can be met with in a summer's day.

THE BAR-ROOM LOAFER.

He lies in bed as long as the happy sunlight, streaming through the window of his unpaid-for lodging-room will permit him, and when he has dressed himself, completed his toilet, and is half satisfied with his personal appearance, he ventures forth.

He has always a certain round to perform, and never did a circuit judge, bent on fulfilling his business with satisfaction to the community, perform his duty with more regularity. He knows, at the first house on his circuit, which he generally reaches by eleven o'clock, that he will meet with Alderman Bluebottle.

Alderman Bluebottle is a stout man, with a hoarse, rough voice, like a raven's. He is popular in his ward, and one of the committee on the alms-house. He is reputed to be pious, and goes dead against the Sunday papers. Attends all corporation and public dinners, and stays till all is *blue*. He drinks a glass of beer at eleven o'clock precisely, to the minute, at precisely the same house every day of his life.

"Sir, the cause of democracy is progressing," says the Alderman.

"Are it?" says a thin, spare man, who accompanies him: he is a tailor by occupation, a man of considerable influence among the cloth, as sharp as a needle, as cutting as a pair of shears, and moreover, a voter in the 21st Ward.

"Are it, though?"

"Yes, sir," says the Alderman, "too long degraded beneath the oppressive exactions of a collapsed, injurious, unsentimental, and prodigal government, as I had the honor to say the other night, in the Board. ('I called for beer, sir:') Sir, what did I say the other night in the board? We were discussing that momentous question, the importance of educating young rats, so as to make them useful for domestic purposes. By the bye, did you hear Mr. Alderman Drinkdry's excellent theory on that subject? All nature informs us, that original minds have lost their distinguishing qualities, and by habit and education, have become the reverse of what they were. Sir, if the human race have done this ere thing, why may not the animal creation. Rats, who now tear up the floors of our dwellings, and ravages our barns, who enter, without feelings of decency and respect, the bed-rooms of our wives and daughters, break into our shops and destroy our property, may, by education, be brought to be protectors, instead of deceivers, and in place of calling out, 'Behold the dust that hangs upon their bloody track,' we may have to shout hosannahs to 'Waiter, bring me some beer.'"

"Yes, sir, to what?"

"To what, sir."

"Yes, sir, to what?"

"To the triumphant march of the rats, while the deep diapason of caterwauling will swell the scenes. Sir, I move the establishment of ten normal schools, for the education of young rats."

While this is going on, our worthy friend, the loafer, has been perusing the papers: he has looked through the Courier and Express, turned up his nose at the Journal of Commerce, requested a gentleman to make haste with the Aurora, and wondered when the Evening Tattler would be out. He is now engaged in reading the bill of the New York Museum. He finishes the bill as Alderman Bluebottle closes his speech, and bowing and simpering, walks forward.

"Good morning, Alderman, what prospects have we for the election."

"Well, sir, really I don't know; I guess it's all O. K."

"I think so too. I have voted in the 21st Ward every year till now. I'm sorry to move. I really think I shall go back."

"The 21st Ward is an excellent Ward, and our people may be useful there. Pray, sir, are you drinking anything?"

"No, Alderman, but as it's you, a very small glass of brandy and water. Now, not too much. Stay, I'll mix it myself."

And so our friend obtains glass No. 1. Acquaintance after acquaintance drops in, and the bar-room loafer manages as often to be recognized, until he finds some unhappy acquaintance, who, in pity to his hungry looks, asks him to dine. And so from day to day and from hour to hour he continues to live, and fret his hour upon the stage.

ANTIQUITIES AND PRODUCTS GINERALLY.

We now come to the ancient diskiveries proper, and the products of the sile. You may here see a piece of the ginooine Plymouth rock. It was thought at one time that

the English had carried it off, and made it a part of the rock of Gibraltar, but when they paid us a visit in red uniform, and tested the material, they found the old stun there, and they found it a Gibraltar tew. *T* was a great letter among the ancients, and from it arose the society of *T* totallers. Their idol, the *Tea*, became so common, arter a spell, that it was emptied by the box-full intew Boston harbor. Turtle, a shell of which you may see in my collection, gave birth tew the sayin' of "shell out." The tarm hierology, which we use in describin' these things, means that the people in old times were ruther toploftical. A number of these matters hev been hard tew diskiver, but they are easy when you know 'em. Now, many on you b'lieve the old sayin' that matches were made in heaven, but I kin prove they were made in New England, 'specially the Lucifer ones. Ef I had time I might say suthin' about the brimstun at one eend of 'em, but I leave you all tew find eout about that, herearter, yourselves. Putty is a great antiquity. Its fluctuation in this day is a remarkable contrast tew the past: putty, anciently, jest stuck where it was put. You hev heern of *corn?* Well, I guess you hev. Tew vary eour subject, and teck things ginerally, we will pass on tew corn, and that brings us tew products. The race anterior tew the ancient Pilgrims knew suthin' abeout this vegetable, but it was left tew eour airly ancestors tew develop the full usefulness of this grain. The Ingins knew heow to use it in the rough, but, oh! Johnny cakes and corn juice, tew what parfection it was finally brought by the descendants of the primitive fathers. This cartouche will show you the tew stages of *corn.*

Here you hev corn in the rough,

Corn.

Corn Juice.

And here you hev it in parfection.

Findin' that by poundin' the grain, mixin' with it a leetle milk and a few eggs, that it made a mixtur of a humanizin' character for the innards, they set tew work tew fix a liquid mixtur eout of the juice, tew was' down the cakes, and pursuin' it through a *spirit* of resarch, from one diskivery tew anuther, they got eout a juice which set their tongues workin' very lively. Findin' it a warmin' mixtur, they kept on takin' it, and finally their legs got tew movin' in sech a zig-zag fashion, that many were shocked with the new drink. This diskivery, undoubtedly, pinted many intu very crooked ways, and gin rise tew the expression that—"This is a great country."

It may be proper, before proceedin' farther, tew state that, the ancient New Englanders wore a becomin' kiverin' in airly times. We hev here a cartouche, presentin' the outline of an early settler, and his descendant of the present gineration. The difference in the outer kiverin' will strike

your eye in a minnit. In old times they went in for an all-sufficient amount of brim, while neow, hevin' grown cute, and savin' of stuff, they cut it so precious narrow, that it is eenamost all shaved off. *Y-e-s* they dew. In the coat some difference may be diskivered ; the antique, as you see, wraps the hull body—while in t'other the body is neglected, and the material is all consigned tew the skirt, or tail-eend of the kiverin'. Frock coats air an exception, and sacks air different and primitive. Here, neow, is a very interestin' relic in the coat way, found in the ruins of an airly

habitation, and it is the best evidence we kin offer, that some of eour Irish friends were among the first native settlers. Let us tech and pass on agin.

It is a gineral opinion that wooden clocks, like some people's larnin', came naturally tew the ancient inhabitants, but who began tew build 'em for exportation remains a hidden mystery. It is pretty sartain, however, that wooden clocks hev ben diskivered, and, I may say, that in my travels, not only on this Continent, but in some furrin' parts, I hev hearn on a few of 'em, and seen a *couple,* I reckon: well, I guess I hev. They are a nat'ral product of New England. Wooden nutmegs spring spontaneously from the sile; tooth-powder is turned out as plenty as saw-dust, and a good deal like it tew; bear's grease made from New England pork, highly scented, is biled down in its factories; and the patent pills, which can cure anything from measles to an amputated head, hev all sprung from this ancient race. I hev here a small cartouche, found in a mortar, which explains pills easy.

Pills.

A fellar is here represented about tew swaller one, and he looks as ef his innards didn't like pills. We hev good reason tew b'lieve that New Englanders made the first shoes, for, on decypherin' one of the old inscriptions below this cartouche, we find inscribed the words :

" *There is nuthin' like leather.*"

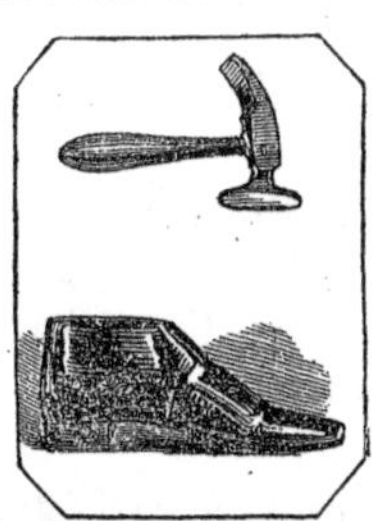

An evidence agin which there kin be no dispute. What a a sublime contemplation it is, that New England protects, by the science of *cobblin,* the gineral understandin' of half creation.

We now come tew the interesting part of eour subject, which more particularly treats of *punkins.* Punkins air indigenous tew our sile, and the ancient settlers feound that eout, at an early period: seeing this big fruit, they natrally sot tew work to see what its innards was made of. By sartain paintin's and cartouches, still presarved, and by written history, as sot deown in hieroglyphics, we learn that they first tried 'em raw, but they didn't eat good, and then they cooked 'em. *Ah!* OH!! AHEM!!! (*licks his chops.*) A diskivery was now made, which sot the mouths of a hull colony watering. They soon got tew making them intew pies, which fact we see proved by this cartouche.

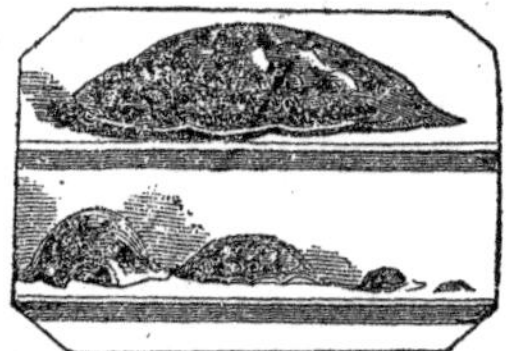

Punkin Pie.

Punkin is put over the pie, to signify that the punkin was first diskivered, and that it was a'ter made intew the pie. You will recollect, that the pie was the second diskivery. The eatin' of the pie wanted no studdy, for it was found, by actual experiment, that ef you put a piece of the pie intew the hands of a Yankee babby, it jest natrally puts it in its mouth.

At one period, we held a deep investigation in the historical society, tew which I hev the honor of bein' Correspondin' Secretary. The subject was this *stun,*

which bore this queer inscription:

ITIS APU NKIN ITIS.

It was plain tew to perceive that it was a petrified vegetable, but it was desp'rate hard tew decipher, *geologically*, its class, 'cause it was so carefully dried up. We sot tew work on the inscription, thinkin' that as it was antique, it would tell the origin of the plant, or gin us a peep intew some matter of airly history. Deacon Starns, the President, a'ter consultin' *all* the books in the library, remarked to the Society, in his commandin' way:—

Deacon.—A'ter a sarchin' hunt, and considerable readin', I hev found eout, that the first word is a Latin tarm. It is—"ITIS,—*thou goest*," and I reckon I wouldn't go through sech anuther hunt tew find eout the beginnin' or eend of creation. I had a sarchin' time, I b'lieve.

Eour antiquary spoke up right peert tew the President on hearin' this:

Antiquary.—Why, Deacon, ITIS, well, *yes*, guess it is, well, I declare, who'd thought it,—and I swow ef the last word don't spell jest the same thing. *Thou goest.* Yes, jest the same. Mabbe the middle means that tew, let me see. No, for spell it which way you will, up or *down*, it seems tew mean suthin' else, y-e-s, I guess it does; well, *really*. I move Deacon, we sit on this stun till we find it eout. Parseverance will dew it, for by that you hev already diskivered the first, and me the last word.

Deacon.—*You* diskiver? *ahem!* You! I found both out myself.

Antiquary.—You will own, Mr. President, that *you* ony named the first.

Deacon.—Yes; and that was the key tew the second, sir: neow how do you feel?

ANTIQUARY.—I reckon, deacon, it's one thing tew find the key, and anuther tew know its use. I aint goin' tew be robbed of my resarches, *I guess;* particularly, a'ter I hev unlocked a secret of sech importance.

DEACON.—Ef the antiquity gentleman of this *so-ci-e-ty* hes a mind tew, he will *please* come tew order.

The society unanimously called the antiquary tew order, and rite off, a new member, a timid lookin' young feller, remarked:

NEW MEMBER.—Ef it would please the society, I would like to make a slight *re*mark; not that I kin throw light upon the subject afore you, a timely *re*mark, however, might lead to new remarks, and *re*markin' upon one point a'ter anuther, would draw eout remarks.

DEACON.—(*Waving hand.*) Go on, sir; let us hear your *remark*, and ef you please make it remarkable brief.

NEW MEMBER.—Yes, sir. I would ony remark, that eour doctor remarked, that *APU*, if the *U* was an *O*, would be the Greek word for *from*.

The sensation at heerin' this was tremenjus. I may say the hull society was set a bilin'. The new member got frightened at what he had did, and I natrally expected him tew run. Eour antiquary moved that a medal be struck in his honor, and that frightened him wus. He said he be durned if they should strike him with a medal, and threatened he'd lick the antiquary the first time he caught him sarchin' in the ruins of his daddy's mill. Finally, the twitter in which they had all been put, smoothed down, and they all, ginerally, sot tew work, tew find eout the last undiskivered word. I told 'em now, myself, that ef the third word had an (*a*) and (*n*) atween the (*n*) and (*k*), I'd think it was *nankin.*

Antiquary.—That's it. It's named a'ter *nankin trowsers!*

President.—Ah! yes, yes; that is a Chinese word. I have heard the captin' of one of my vessels say it was a teown in China. Ah! ha! that is it, sure enough, I reckon. Well, I cal'late the hull reads now, clear as moonshine: let me see:

Latin.	*Greek.*	*Chinese.*	*Latin.*
ITIS	APU	NKIN	ITIS.
THOU GOEST	FROM	NANKIN,	THOU GOEST.

It is plain as the nose on a face, tew the eye of science ginerally, and tew this society in particular, that this stun was once a Chinese fruit, sent eout to this country, to see ef it would *fructify*, and here the darn thing has taken a notion instead to *petrify!*

The applause was tremenjus!

Zachariah Stanhope, a consarned dirty little rascal, who swept our historical room and made the fires, bust right eout intew a snigger. He had been sticking his tow head atween the heads of the society, and was deciphering the inscription tew.

President.—Zack, what air you sniggerin' eout in that way abeout, eh?

Zach.—At the stun, sir.

President.—Well, what abeout the stun?

Zach.—At the *words*, sir.

President.—Hah! At the words, eh? Well, what do you spell eout of them? come, let us hear you; and the president winked at the society.

Zach,—(a'ter wiping his nose, and lickin' his lips, read right eout,)—

IT-IS-A-PUNKIN-IT-IS!!

And so it was, a consarned dried up, petrified punkin, that had dried up, as you kin see, more one way than t'other. A'ter votin' a medal to the diskiverer of this inscription, eour society adjourned.

Ladies and gentlemen, walk up and see my antiquities.

I do not claim for Mr. Hill any great originality, either in the conception or execution of the following lecture on the antiquities of New England. I feel almost sure the idea was suggested by Mr. Gliddon's lectures on Egypt, to which it bears a strong resemblance in the very extraordinary character of the facts related, and the oddity of the hypothesis sought to be established. The title of Mr. Hill's lecture, viz. "Antiquities of New England," brings to my mind a question once absolutely put to me by a physician, then practising in the city of Brooklyn. I was walking along the Heights with him one evening, when the Doctor turned towards, and thus addressed me, "Doctor," said he, "are all those old, ancient antiquities of former times, all covered with *ivory*, which we read of in England, realities or mere creatures of the imagination?" It will appear almost incredible, perhaps, that a man possessing a diploma for the practice of a liberal profession, could deliver himself of "such perilous stuff;" but I pledge my word that the language I have put into his mouth is verbatim, that which he employed to express himself on this occasion. With regard to Mr. Hill's *Antiquities* of *New* England, I shall leave my reader to judge whether "they are realities, or mere creatures of the imagination."

THE PEOPLE AND ANTIQUITIES OF NEW ENGLAND, YANKEEOLOGICALLY SPEAKING.

It is a pooty ginerally conceded fact, that man is a queer critter, and that when he aint movin' abeout he's doin' suthin' else. This pint bein' conceded, we pass on tew remark, that the first race which sot deown in New England, were of this movin', reound kind of critters, and I rekon they hev fixed a leetle mite of their stirrin' reound propensities upon the ginerations that followed a'ter. This part of eour subject may not account for the milk in the cocoa nut, but it does account for why your humble sarvint is here. All owin' tew his New England propensity for stirrin' reound. Well, hevin' settled this pint we'll pass on tew consider the next. It has been ginerally thought, that the airly inhabitants of New England all came from some place, and I guess they did. What's more, they found a place tew come tew, when they came. This in some measure, accounts for the ancient sayin', that "you'll be there when you git tew the place." Well, a'ter eatin' a *clam-chowder*, of which we have sufficient evidence that they were desp'rately fond, 'cause the shells air scattered abeout promiscuously, these airly New Englanders sot to work at makin' themselves tew *hum*, and they succeeded a'ter a fashion. The fashion hes ben found to be a tolerable good one tew, for their posterity stick tew the same way of gittin' along, even unto the present generation. Well, as I was sayin', they made themselves at *hum*. Where they landed, there was considerable sand, some stuns, and a leetle dash of water, and from sartin' hieroglyphical evidence, we air enabled tew make out, that they were jest abeout as hard-headed a race as ever made up their minds tew settle down wherever they had a mind tew. It aint exactly known whether they came in a *hickory* canoe, or a *birch* basket, but jedgin' from the way New England schoolmasters use these tew kind of woods, eour historical society hev settled deown intew the opinion, that they came in both. Select men were chosen and appinted in them days to rule over the people, and they in turn used tew select some of the people tew be ruled over, and they ginerally did this rulin' with a rod. In modern New England varsion, the select men air "old flints," I reckon 'cause some on' em air a leetle flinty-hearted. Talkin' of flints brings me tew an important pint in my subject, and that is ROCKS. Nigh ontew all on you hev heerd abeout the *Rock of Plymouth*, and if you hev'nt, it's a darned shame for it's often enough talked about. The ancient inhabitants of New England, beyond dispute, landed on this rock, and they found it a pooty solid, *steady* kind of a footin'. From this fact grew eout the common sayin' that New-England is the land of *steady habits*. Heow could they be otherwise, when they commenced on so solid a foundation? Without runnin' this rock intew the ground, I'd like tew say suthin' abeout its *antiquity*. It is pooty ginerally conceded that afore it was diskivered, it had staid in the same place a pooty long spell—mabbe anterior to Adam! Who knows? I'll be durned if I dew. All I know, and all it's necessary for me tew find eout is, that it is *there*, and I ruther guess, a'ter I hev handled it a leetle mite *there*, I'll leave it. You see here, in this diagram, a correct representation, or as nigh as I can git it, of this identical rock, (*Lecturer points at it,*)

and if you all look sharp, you will see that it is pooty considerable of a stun. It is known tew be, by a kind of natural humin cal'lation, an all-sufficient sight older than the Egyptian pyramids, and anterior tew the present times, at least 5000 years. Our society aint ben able, as yet, tew trace the Polk name down tew the airly dynasties of the *select* men, but I reckon we will yet find it eout. We hev, however, in eour archilogical diggin' diskivered the word *Pillow,* but whether it was any relation tew *Gideon Pillow,* is not yet sartin.' The word is thought tew hev a soft meanin,' but larnin tew read hieroglyphics, we hev ascertained that a man named Jacob, who was lost in the wilderness, *pillowed* upon a *stun.* Now, *Gideon* bein' also ancient, a spirit of deduction natrally leads us tew *Pillow* and then Jacob pints eout the *stun,* and here, you see, we slide right back tew *rock* from where we started. This explanation, we think, fully establishes this cartouche, which has been whittled in the old stun by a son of the airly Pilgrims.

This is the first indication we hev of the tune " Yankee Doodle," and the sound on it is explained by the steps and crow of a rooster, thus: " Yan—kee—doo—del—dan—dy. One—two—three—four—*ooo!* (crow.) The *Arabs,* by which we mean the modern portion on 'em, used to visit Plymouth Rock, and break off pieces of the stun,

Yankee-Doodle-Doo.

eout of which propensity grew the common saying, "I'd a good deal ruther crack rock." Antiquarians, tew, visited the old spot, and used tew fill their pockets with pieces of the stun, which give rise tew the modern expression, "sech a fellar is in town with *a pocket full of rocks.*' You kin see this symbolized in this cartouche.

Rock.

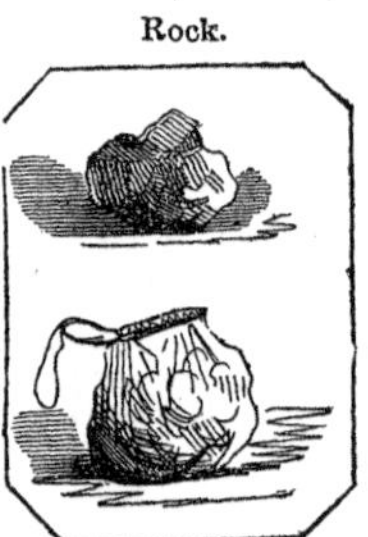

Pocket full of Rocks.

The next *stun,* or I should say pile of stuns, is the Monument, and usin' the words of a celebrated New-England Savan, "*there it stands!*"

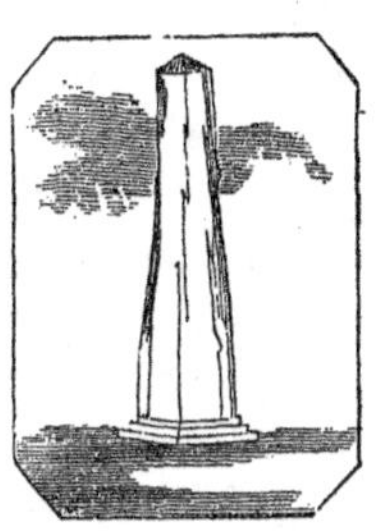

and you couldn't, very easy, make it dew anythin' else. It is situated on Bunker Hill, named after old *Joe Bunker,* who used tew make shoes rite down at the hill *foot.* Whether the rest of the spot and *Hills* in gineral were named arter my own ancesters, I aint yet diskivered, but in future explorations I hev hopes of findin' eout, on some *Hill,* a key-stun pinting eout the gratifyin' fact that your lecturer is descended from a ginooine *old settler.* *When* this obelisk began tew be histed up, is a period only known to the "oldest inhabitant." Sartain curious inscriptions, buried in a hollow stun beneath its base, tells all abeout it, but I aint seen 'em, nor I don't expect tew soon do, but I know they are there, 'cause somebody told me. Here is a miniature of it, whittled eout in my smoothest style. The great distinguishin' featur' about this stupendous mountain of stun is the fact, that they begun tew fix it *up* from the top *down.* I guess now, mabbe some on you don't b'lieve this, but ef I could ony git you all intew a mesmeric state you'd see it jest as *easy*—I might say, jest as easy as ef you had your eyes shet. Some dew say that clairvoyance is a regular "open and shet;" heow that is, I leave you tew cypher eout by your own natral bent of genius, while I proceed tew explain heow the Bunker Hill obelisk was built downward. From a cute and sarchin' investigation, I hev diskivered that the hull pile of rock is capped by one *stun.* Now, heow could the pile be put up under that stun? I reckon we hev neow arriv at the pint of the subject. As I said before, it is not one stun, but a whole pile—now, there you hev it—how is it going to git up? By the simple process (simple when you know it,)—and there it is, jest like Zacharia Dempson's new patent machine for manufacturin' the wind intew *short-cake,* by the simple process of mesmerism, the top stun, and making it stay there, at jest the height they wanted—tew elevate the pile above the airth. This diagram shows the slantin' of the mesmeric fluid, and here you see the top stone.

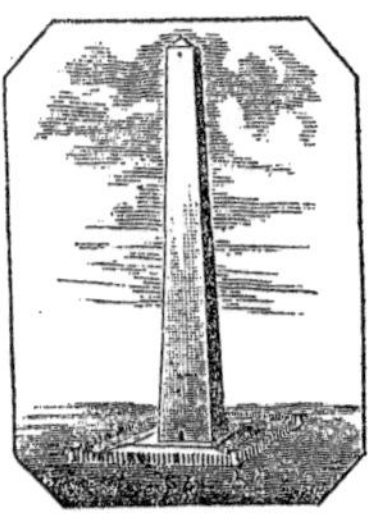

There is another streak of fluid on the other side which you can't see, but you can see easy that when the mesmeric power could hold this stun up here, it was desp'rate easy tew hitch the other stuns tew the fluid, and by drawin' your hand down so, (*manipulates,*) stick 'em so consarned fast that an airthquake couldn't shake 'em loose. I don't wonder some of you opin your eyes, for the progress of this age, in the onward march of antiquarian research, new diskiveries, and everlastin' upturnin' of new things, keep continually putting the cap-stun on all preconceived notions. I would jest refer you,—and this pile is an astounding illustration of the *re*-markable difference atween the ancient New Englanders, and the ancient Egyptians. It'll strike you in a moment, and it'll show you what a dark and be-nighted set they were, as you get east'ard, while as you get west'ard, as far as the eastern part of this continent, it'll be diskivered that mankind grew cute and cunnin'—*y-e-s* they did! The poor yaller-skinned Asiatics, had no more sense,—I swow, I've a propensity tew bust rite intew a reglar roar, when I think that a people who looked so ripe as to be yaller, could be so durnation green. Would you b'lieve it?—I reckon you'll find it hard tew—these be-nighted people writ deown the history of their monaments rite on their face, jest where every fellar who tuck the trouble tew larn, could read it right eout in meetin', ef he'd a mind tew. I say, they writ it right deown on the stun, so it couldn't be wasked eout with the rain of centuries. Neow you can see the Egyptin' darkness of these poor critters. Heow is it on t'other side? Heow, and what distinguishes the ancient New England monament builders? What shows their cuteness? I kin tell you in a few words, pertinently delivered. The New Englanders buried the history of their monaments in the solid rock, under the hull pile of *stun*, and if the futur' sarcher a'ter ancient New England antiquities, wants tew read it, he'll hev tew either know mesmerism, or else pull the hull tremenjus obelisk, cap-stun and all, deown, tew find out what it's all about. This is what I call cute. It is showin' tew the world that the pryin', sneekin' reound, findin' eout propensities of futur' ginerations will hev to scratch and a few, afore they can git intew their secrets.

We now come tew anuther head of our lectur', and that is HEARTH-STUNS.

This last named antiquity has sometimes appeared in *brick*, and then agin in *marble*; but who found the *last brick* thrown in, or *at* this head of our discourse, eour society aint yet decided upon. Where the hearth-stun lay, however, and what were its gineral uses, is jest as well known tew eour society, as the big letters in the New England Primer. You hev here, in this cartouche, a rude representation of the *hearth-stun*.

How the inhabitants made use of this stun, is the subject we shall talk on for a spell. I cal'late it was in pooty constant use. Hieroglyphics relate that Deacon Bigelow was seated, one evenin' about nine o'clock, on this side; and on t'other side, jest about there, old Mrs. Bigelow was sittin' smokin'. A leetle tew the right of Mrs. B., and jest, I may say, in her shadder, was seated Abby, the eldest darter, who has jest got in from singin'-school; and rite opposite tew her is Jedediah Peabody, a spruce, smart-lookin' young fellar, son of old Deacon Peabody, who has ben seein' Nabby hum from the singin' class. Jest abeout there, frontin' the fire, is seated the deacon's *eleventh* child and as he is the *last*, of course he is a pet. He kin jest talk plain, and seein' Jed come in with Abby, his eves are abeout as wide open, as it could be expected any young critter's would stretch at his tender years. He sees Jed wink at Abby, (*Oh!*) and now he watches Abby, and sees her look pleased, and shake her head at Jed. (*Good gracious!*) And so he eyes one, and then t'other, his astonishment growin' on him every minnit, until his Ma says:

MRS. B.—Deacon Bigelow is the cattle critters fed?

DEACON.—(*Sleepy*)—Well, I reckon Isaiah has gin 'em suthin', and afore this litter'd 'em down.

MRS. B.—Is the kindlin' wood brought in tew?

DEACON.—Yes, *y-e-s*, my dear, all is r-i-

MRS. B.—Then come along, git up and let us go tew bed. You, Abby, mind you kiver the fire up, and fasten the door afore you come tew bed; and you, Jed, it's time you were tew hum. Gideon, git up, my child, and dew let us all git tew bed.

Off they go, and eout in the hall little Gid commences tew blow on Abby.

GIDEON.—Ma, you ourt tew take your birch tew Jed Peabody.

MA.—Why, my dear boy, what did Jed dew?

GIDEON—He kept all the time makin' mouths at Abby?

DEACON.—Toddle along Gid, and shet up.

GIDEON.—Shet up! I guess I seed him dew wus than that; he bit her the other night right on her lips, I seed him, so I did.

We will neow return tew the hearth-stun. Jed has ben hitchin' his cheer 'round tew Abby, and by hieroglyphical devices we larn that he gits his cheer chuck up agin hers, and by the progressive rule by which we decypher the first part, we conclude that Jed has ben at it agin, the durned critter has ben kissin' on her, or as young Gid calls it, bitin' her on the lips agin.

From the blue-book *papyrus,* presarved as a relic of the reg'lar old mummys who first gathered round Plymouth rock, we larn that kissin' was so prevalent in the airly days of New England, that the young folks were at it, not only only on every day in the week, but Sunday tew; and, therefore, it was found necessary tew put a stop tew it on the seventh, by law. I reckon that, like in modern times, the young folks among the ancients sot Sunday aside as a day upon which to dew up pooty considerable of that interestin' kind of labor.

The hearth of every true New Englander reveres this *hearth-stun,* for around it, no matter whether it be of brick or marble, gethers the loved associations of hum. It is endeared to him by the memory of a venerated father, the fond care of a gentle mother, the sweet love of a bright-eyed sister, or the manly friendship and affection of a brother. In infancy he has crowed with glee at the bright blaze which flashed from its surface—in youth he has listened in wonder, beside it, to the related history of his Puritan ancestors—in manhood he has whispered a tale of love in the ear of beauty, by the border of this old hearth-stun, and sealed on the fair lips of virtue, the pledge of unending attachment, and in old age, on Thanksgiving Day, he has gathered around it his children and his children's children, and like a patriarch of old, thanked his Creator that he lived to hear again the sweet music of his kindred's voices. The hieroglyphic seal of this old stun is inscribed on the heart's tablet of every ginooine Yankee.

LECTURE ON NEW ENGLAND.

WHO can read the *simple history* of the Republic of North America, without emotions of the most pious reverence and deep affection? With the improvements in modern navigation, it is now an *every-day affair* to see vessels that have traversed the widest seas; but think of things as they were *then*, the vague ideas of this "wilderness world," its *savage* inhabitants, and its beasts of prey, that were the horrors of the nursery, as are those now of Africa and Australasia, and you can form some conception of the feelings of fathers and their families, on exiling themselves from *home*, and all that was *dear* on earth, save their *sacred faith*; that, like St. John in the Isle of Patmos, they might find some ritual in a *distant* wild. Our forefathers came to these shores under convoy of no *naval* armament; they brought no trophies of glory; they were not attended with the pomp and pageantry of the *military adventurer*, but with the "simple scrip and staff of the pilgrim;" unlike the founders of *ancient Rome*, they were not a set of *outlaws* and fugitive *felons*, but a company of Christian *brethren*, with their wives and children, led on by no grovelling *cupidity* or *worldly ambition*, but by unfaltering devotion and faith. With *such* an *ancestry* and history, with institutions calculated to develop the *highest* dignity of character, with a *country* possessing *every* thing in the *physical* and *moral* world, to *enlarge* the mind, what will be the ultimate bound of our attainments as a people?

A few days since, as I stood upon the top of yonder capital, *the crown* of this goodly city, gazing upon the picturesque panorama of which it is the centre, its hive of human habitations, its spires, its streets teeming with a countless and stirring multitude, its hum of business, its wharves and shipping, its green common and drooping elms, the only remnants of verdure's former realm, its bay gemmed with islands and whitened with sails, expanding into the ocean; and when I turned to the numerous villages, in every direction, clustering around their churches, like flocks around their shepherds; the different rail-roads with their trains, like some fabled monsters, exhaling smoke and fire, and apparently perforating hills, and flying over valleys, the naval citadel bearing that flag which, though unfurled but a few years ago, is now respected in every sea,—I was lost in rapture, as my mind pictured the *probable* scene but *two* centuries ago. On the height where this building is based, has the Indian hunter paused awhile, to contemplate this picture of nature, and could he have expressed himself in the language of the poet, he would have exclaimed,

> "I am monarch of all I survey!"

Where stands this proud and noble city, was then an unbroken forest, with here and there a thin wreath of smoke, betraying the *nestling wigwam;* the partridge led the young, where now the *Christian mother* watches the gambols of her children—the beautiful *fawn* sported where the *artless girl* winds her way to school, and the *cooing pair* built their little home in the branches beneath which *bashful love* now *woos* and *wins* the *fair* and *pure.* Where the thrush made the common "air most musical," now swells the pealing anthem of the choir and the organ; the church-bell tolls the knell of every parting hour where the screams of the panther, and the howl of the wolf, once alarmed the ear of night; where the eloquence of Webster, Everett, Choate, and Bancroft, are like household tones, was then heard the harangue of some *aboriginal orator;* the bay which now bears the steamer and the ship, was then unrippled save by the light canoe and the "black duck with her glossy breast swinging silently" on the glassy heaving surge.

Alas, for the poor red man! He has gone with his game to the fair hunting-grounds of the West; his last arrow is spent; his bow is broken; the hand that twanged its string has forgotten its cunning. A new race and a new scene have sprung up as by some strange miracle.

If so short a time has made so vast an alteration, what will it be two centuries hence? it is not in the power of man to foretell; may *each* generation advance the embellishment and refinement of this Athens of America, and its greatness be as enduring as the Acropolis. The true greatness of a state has been justly said to consist in the character of its people.

Men, *high-minded* men,
With powers as far above dull brutes endued
In forest, brake, or den,
As beasts excel cold rocks and brambles rude:
Men who their *duties know*,
But know their *rights*, and *knowing* dare maintain,
Present the long-aimed blow,
And crush the *tyrant* while they *rend* the *chain*,
These constitute a *State*.

Though New England cannot boast of rich plantations, and gangs of laborers producing vast crops of cotton, corn, and rice, of inexhaustible mines and rich prairies, waving like lakes of verdure, nor of *many* fields glistening with the golden wheat, yet, like the mother of the Gracchii, she can point to her *children* and say, " *These are my jewels* "— " here is my wealth." Can you show me those who are fairer, braver, or *smarter* than these ?

When asked by Madame de Stael, " Who is the greatest woman in the empire?" Napoleon is said to have replied, " She who is the mother of the most children." If this be true, New England will be apt to bear off the palm, for this is her great *staple of produce*, and in its *quantity* she can vie with any other mother in the world, not excepting Ireland, to say nothing of its *quality*. She can point you also to her battle-fields, and the graves of those who have fallen on the field, or the deck, or have devoted their interests, their wealth, and their lives, to the good of their race and their country. She will show you her churches, her colleges, her school-houses, her benevolent associations, her marts, villages, and hamlets, her neat farms, where art and industry are triumphing over nature, her factories, founderies, and workshops, where human ingenuity is contriving to lighten the load of labor, and by giving new value to matter, promote the comfort and refinement of man. She will there show you *her slaves*, of which it cannot be said as of the lilies, " they toil not, neither do they *spin* ;" but her right of ownership cannot be questioned, as they are *hers* by *discovery*—*machines* of her own contrivance, and for which she has her *patent* from Washington. She will show you her ships, whose keels cleave every navigable sea; her long list of distinguished men, her enterprising and thorough merchants, and wherever the foot of civilized man has ever trod, she will show you a representative.

Land of the forest and the rock,
Of dark blue lake and mighty river,
Of mountains rear'd aloft to mock
The storm's career, the ligntning's shock,
My own green land for ever.

Land of the beautiful and brave,
The freeman's home, the martyr's grave,
The nursery of giant men,
Whose deeds have linked with every glen,
And every hill, and every stream,
The romance of some warrior dream;
Oh, never may a *son* of thine,
Where'er his wandering steps incline,
Forget the sky which bent above
His childhood, like a dream of love,
The stream beneath the *green* hill glowing,
The broad-armed trees above it growing,
Or *hear* unmoved the *taunt of scorn*,
Breathed *o'er* the *brave* New-England born.

There is no one concerning whom there have been such conflicting opinions as the native of this region; he has been compared to the Scotchman, whom he resembles in many particulars, but mingled with these some qualities of the Englishman, and more that are peculiarly his own. He can truly be called *an original.* This is manifested not only in his own inventive genius, but in his *individuality* as a man. Wherever you behold him there is something about him different from those of other origin. It is not fair to judge him by other men, for he is *sui generis.* If the Virginian excels as an advocate, the New Englander is distinguished as a counsellor. He is the founder of new States and the framer of their laws. As a public speaker, he is more remarkable for sound argument than a playful fancy. He is more distinguished as a profound statesman than a mere politician, and makes Demosthenes, rather than Cicero, his model. When those from other sections are apt to act in concert, in the councils of the nation, you find him consulting his own conscience, and acting accordingly, regardless of immediate consequences. In sarcasm, he has been unsurpassed, but his favorite weapon is the sledge-hammer, rather than the rapier; though equable and cool in temper, when once aroused, he is like a *lion at bay*. He has been reproached with a want of imagination, yet he has the honor to claim a large majority of our *national poets*, and among them those who, at home and abroad, have held the highest rank.. As a philosopher, he believes in that individual freedom "which protects itself against the usurpations of society; which does not cower to human opinion; which feels itself accountable to a higher tribunal than man's; which respects a higher law than fashion; which respects itself too much to be the slave or tool of the many." As an artist, he is pre-eminent in the higher walks of painting, architecture, and ornamental gardening. As an editor and political writer, he is unequalled. As a merchant, he sends his vessels all over the world, and owns two-thirds of the shipping of his country. He is a first-rate financier, and banks and insurance companies under his direction are apt to preserve their solvency, and *give good dividends* when *others* are bankrupt. In the language of Chevalier, at the north or the south, in the east as well as the west, he is a true Marquis of Carrabas. At Baltimore, as well as at Boston, in New Orleans as well as at Salem, in New York as well as at Portland, if a merchant is mentioned who has made—and kept, by-the-bye a very difficult part of it—a large fortune by sagacity and forecast, you will find that he is a *Yankee.* He will leave his country for the East or West Indies, and after several years absence, return to his native land, erect a splendid villa on the site of the old *homestead,* or select some wooded eminence for his new mansion, and ere long the desert smiles like "Araby the blest." As a *manufacturer,* he was the first to prosecute the business successfully, and has more capital invested in this branch of industry, than all those from other parts of his country together. As a *mechanic,* he is constantly studying to *save labor* and money. He was the first to suggest to Fulton the idea of steam navigation, and the first to succeed in propelling vessels in this way. He was the inventor of the *cotton-gin,* which has done more for the culture of cotton and consequent wealth of the South, than all else together; to use the language of the popular author we before have quoted, "but for him the vast cotton plantations of the South would still be an uncultivated waste." He is the projector of *new towns* and *internal improvements,* and the *principal constructor* on all our *public works.* He builds *navies* and *ordnance* for the Sultan of Turkey, *war-steamers* for the Autocrat of Russia, *machinery for the Emperor of Austria,* whale-boats and whaling-gear for the King of France, and locomotive *engines* for *England,* the *boasted workshop* of the world. He is in more than one sense a *builder,* and had he lived in the days of Solomon, would no doubt have been a Knight Templar.

Not an acre of land is cultivated in the Union, not a ship floats, not an American book is read, not a meal eaten, a article of clothing prepared, or a bank-note engraved in this Union, that is not more or less the product of Yankee labor and enterprise. As a *farmer*, he does not suffer himself to be outdone; he not only invents the best ploughing, planting, mowing, raking, cradling, thrashing, shelling, winnowing, and *grinding* machines, but he is the best agricultural editor, and is pretty sure to take the premium for the fattest oxen and pigs, the finest cheese and butter, largest squashes and pumpkins, in all cattle-shows. He also displays great skill in subduing the wilderness, raises his log cabin at the falls of St. Antony, displaces the colony of the beaver, to make room for his saw-mill on the Upper Missouri. As a *sailor* and a *soldier*, our naval and military history will speak in abler language than I can command. He was the first to cross the Atlantic in a *steamer;* shoot seals at the South Shetlands, and slay the sea-elephant at Kergulan's Land; catch cod at Labrador, and whale at Delago Bay; was the first to discover, and as yet the only one who has ever landed upon the Southern polar continent. He takes a peep, by way of curiosity, into the mælstrom, and would, for a sufficient inducement to warrant the outlay, contrive to solve the polar problem, and look into Symmes' Hole. He hails the Russian exploring expedition when rejoicing at the discovery of a new group of islands in the Antarctic Ocean, and inquires if they *don't want a pilot?* On being asked who he is, and where he is from, gives his name as Captain Nat. Palmer, of the sloop Hero of 60 tons burthen, from Stonington, Connecticut. The Yankee is, in short, a *universal genius;* his native soil is remarkable for its stubborn and sterile roughness, and he can be compared to the oak of his own rocky hills; strongly and deeply are rooted his principles and habits; if he has not the grace of the Southern palmetto, he has more of that hardy strength which can wrestle with the rude storms of life. Like the young eagle reared on the lightning-rifted cliff, he partakes of the same spirit of fierce independence and aspiration, looks unawed upon the storms that rage around him, and though on soaring wing he may wander leagues away, he is sure to return to the nestling-place of his attachment.

They love the land because it is their own,
  And scorn to give the reason why;
A stubborn race, fearing and flattering none,
  Such are they nurtured, and such they die.
All but a few apostates meddling
With merchandise, pounds, shillings, pence, and *peddling*,
Or wandering through the Southern countries, teaching
  The A, B, C, or Webster's spelling-book,
Gallant and godly, making love, and preaching,
  And gaining, by what they call "hook and crook,"
And what *moralists* call *over-reaching*,
  A *decent living*. The Virginians look
Upon them with as favorable eyes
  As Gabriel on the devil in paradise;
But these are but their outcasts—view them near,
  At home where all their worth and pride is placed,
And then their hospitable fire burns clear,
  And there the lowliest farm-house hearth is graced
With manly hearts in piety sincere.
Faithful in love, in honor stern and chaste,
In friendship warm and true, in danger brave—
Beloved in life and sainted in the grave.

He has more of steady courage than of romantic chivalry and impulse. With no other patrimony than a trade, or an education, he early feels the pressure of that strongest inducement to action, *stern necessity,* and does not look for many examples in his own acquaintance of *self-made men* to stimulate and guide him. He is taught in the home of frugality, that "a penny saved is a penny earned," and learns in his school-book that "tall oaks from little acorns grow." He feels the importance of gradually adding to his fund of wealth and knowledge; is apt before embarking in any adventure to *count the cost,*" and is more remarkable as a shrewd and safe operator than an improvident speculator; yet he has no objection to laying out his farm into *town lots,* but is rather apt to sell before there is a fall in the market. He possesses a great deal of common sense, as well as brass, and is remarkable for his *general information.* More inquisitive than communicative, and is celebrated for picking up knowledge by the wayside; he is ever seeking something new, and how he can turn it to *profitable* account; rather reserved and suspicious, when appearances are not marked *O. K.*, but clinches those whom judgment has once approved with "hooks of steel;" he is the true alchymist, for he possesses the power of converting the *baser* metal into *gold,* and the divining *rod* held in his hand is pretty sure to point out the *hidden ore.* Regarding cash as the *primum mobile,* he acts upon the principle that there is "no friendship in trade," and is therefore a *keen fellow* at a bargain; yet when he has once amassed a fortune, he richly endows literary and charitable institutions, and is kind to the poor.

It has been our misfortune to be judged too much by hawking pedlers, who make the "rule of three" their "golden rule," and the arithmetic their creed. I once knew two individuals who set up in trade together in a western village. After looking over the ground, they concluded that it was best for one to join a certain church, the other a certain *political party*, and they turned up a copper to see which each should join. He has the convenient capability of adapting himself to every situation, and it has been said, that if you place him on a rock in the midst of the ocean, with a penknife and a bundle of shingles, he would manage to work his way ashore. He sells salmon from Kennebec to the people of Charleston; haddock, *fresh*, from Cape Cod to the planters of Matanzas, raises coffee in Cuba, swaps mules and horses for molasses in Porto-Rico, retails ice from Fresh Pond, in Cambridge, to the East Indians—mutton, from Brighton, at New Orleans and South America; and *manufactures* morus multicaulis for the Governor of Jamaica; becomes an admiral in foreign navies; starts in a cockle-shell craft of fifteen tons burden, loaded with *onions*, *mackerel*, and other notions, too numerous to mention, for Valparaiso; baits his traps on the Columbia River; catches wild beasts in Africa, for Macomber and Co's "Grand Caravan;" sells granite on contract to rebuild San Juan de Ulloa—is ready, like Ledyard, to start for Timbuctoo to-morrow morning—exiles himself for years from his home, to sketch in their own wilderness the "wild man of the woods," and astonishes refined Europe with the seeming presence of the untutored savage. When introduced to Metternich, he asks him "What's the news?" says "How do you do, marm," to Victoria; and prescribes "Thompson's eye-water" to the mandarins of China!

He is found foremost among those who sway the elements of society; is the schoolmaster for his country, and missionary to the *whole* heathen *world*.

He is unequalled in tact, and instead of travelling round about ways, starts "across lots" for any desired point.

He has come nearer to the discovery of perpetual motion than any other man; and if ever *it* is made, we *guess* he will be the lucky chap to do it. He is the man to

> Bid harbors open, public ways extend,
> Bid temples worthy of his God ascend;
> Bid the broad arch the dangerous flood contain—
> The mote projecting, break the roaring main;
> Back to his bounds the subject sea command,
> And roll obedient rivers through the *land.*

I cannot close this lecture without addressing a few words to the women of New-England. Her beaming eyes and charming smiles remain to awaken and reward the pulsations of patriotism; her affection and tenderness solaced and sustained the fainting pilgrim; and in the days that tried men's souls, she gave confidence to the desponding, and energy to the weak; her kind hand assuaged the sufferings of the wounded, and her bosom pillowed the head of the dying.

Whether as a wife, a mother, a sister, or a friend, she has the strongest claims upon our affection and gratitude, and holds, of social enjoyment, the golden key. She first implants the lessons of piety, and garlands our home with flowers of love and bliss; she is the guardian angel of our lives, and guides our feet to purity and peace. I will not say more at this time, than that there is nothing which more clearly marks the degree of refinement among a people than the station of "Heaven's last best gift;" and we can add, that there is no part of the world, where, with all classes she commands the high respect, and exerts the influence that she does in New-England.

CHIPS FROM SARATOGA.

SARATOGA, in the fashionable season, perhaps presents the best menagerie of "human critters" for the study of the curious, of any other place in the United States. Not only is the animal, man, there seen in the greatest variety, but under the most advantageous circumstances for those who are fond of seeing him in the full display of extra-domestic habits and manners. In a place where so large a number assemble from all parts of the United States, from all professions, and from all classes of people as are to be met with in Saratoga, it would be strange if, with some elegance and refinement, there was not a tolerable sprinkling of coarseness and vulgarity; with much of the quiet dignity and repose which characterizes the well-born and the educated, there was not a great deal of ignorant assumption, and contemptible purse-pride. The face of society in this country is continually changing. The high, commanding forehead of to-day, is down in the mouth to-morrow; and the proudly turned-up nose of yesterday, is laid flat by some plebeian fist to-day. The aristocracy of our families seldom lasts beyond a generation or two, and in no place in the United States can you more plainly see the influences of the great democratic principle of equality more savagely struggling to maintain its supremacy than in the fashionable watering-places of the Union. For a season or two, or perhaps three, you may possibly meet the same families, but for the most part in that time you will experience a great change both in the manner and quality of the visitors. The fluctuations in cotton, or the decline of tallow, has produced wonderful changes. Parties who, in your remembrance, were content with a cheap excursion to Coney Island, are now ambitiously apeing the manners of the *ton* at Newport or Saratoga; and those you perhaps envied there, as the observed of all observers, for a few seasons, are now content with a maritime excursion along the shores of Long Island.

Mr. Hill visited Saratoga on many occasions, and always met with a hearty support from the gay loiterers to his evenings' entertainments. I know not what advantage Mr. Hill might have derived from his observation of character on these visits, but I regret to say, he has left very few written records of his experiences. From the nature of the notes he made, and which are now in my possession, it is evident that he intended, at some time or other, to enlarge upon them for future use.

In 1846, Mr. Hill visited Saratoga professionally. On the first day, he went to dinner at the United States Hotel; he was seated opposite a little, round dumpling of a man, whose fat, red face displayed an utter absence of everything like care, and whose happy smile showed, if not the possession of a good heart, a most undeniable integrity of digestion. He was evidently a stranger to those little conventionalisms which distinguish polite society. He was not easy. He fidgetted in his chair, rubbed his hands, wishing, as it appeared, to hide the confusion of his feeling in the exuberant action of his body. He looked up and down the table not a little puzzled to make a choice from the endless variety of dishes upon the table. At length his eye distended, and the smile upon his face became brighter and broader. "Waiter," said he, "are those green peas?"

"Yes, sir."

"What! green peas?"

"Yes, sir."

"Give me some, waiter; don't take them away. I'm very fond of green peas: don't take them away."

"Ah! woodcock, waiter. Is that woodcock?"

"Yes, sir."

"Give me some woodcock, waiter. Don't take them away, waiter: I am very fond of woodcock."

He now set to work upon his woodcock and peas, and whilst busy devouring the luxury, a gentleman acquainted with Mr. Hill, and who sat next our fat friend, said: "I am very happy to see you at the Springs, Mr. Hill."

The little man dropped his knife and fork, and after staring Mr. Hill full in the face for a moment, turned to the gentleman who had spoken, inquired of him "who was that man over there—and what is he—and what does he do?"

"A great many things," replied the other, with a very serious air. He is a great delineator of Yankee character. He can put his face in ten thousand shapes, and imitate the look and manners of every man he meets."

"You don't say so?"

"Yes, sir; he gives an entertainment to-morrow night, and you had better take care what you do or say, or he will show you up in the most laughable style. He has monstrous power."

The little man became at once very serious. He was

not so silly as not to know that he was a little out of place in the company, in which a plethoric purse alone had given him a place, and he dreaded the idea of becoming an object of ridicule. The green peas faded before his eyes, the charms of the woodcock had taken wing and flown away. As soon as possible, after dinner, he sought an opportunity of speaking to Mr. Hill. Approaching to where he stood, he tapped him gently on the shoulder, and drawing him on one side, said: "Look here, Mr. Hill, you are not going to make the folks laugh at me, are you?"

"Make the folks do what at you?"

"Laugh at me."

"Why, what put such an idea into your head?"

"Why I was told you was—you see, Mr. Hill, I'm a kind of strange among these folks here, but at home I am "some pumpkins." Now, I don't mind standing five or six dollars, if you won't say nothing about me. Now, don't, Mr. Hill, won't you?"

"Never fear," said Mr. Hill; "it is not my province nor my nature to pick out individuals, to show them up to ridicule; so there's no fear."

"Well, now, that's hearty; and if that waiter has not taken away the peas and the woodcock, I'll go and finish my dinner." So taking Mr. Hill cordially by the hand, he went on his way rejoicing.

There is a class of young men, who let their dresses wear them, instead of wearing their dresses. They are but, at best, mere human appendages to a given quantity of broadcloth and starch. Classes of the softer sex, if anything can be softer than the male class referred to, are equally liable to be infected with the same weakness. Saratoga abounds with humans of this genus. I do not know that one would care anything about them, if it were not, that, presuming upon the unexceptionable character of their attire, they did not thrust themselves upon one's notice. If they were only endowed with discretion enough to keep their mouths closed, they might pass muster as very respectable lay figures for the use of tailors and milliners, but they seldom have judgment enough for that, and out of their own mouths they stand condemned.

On one occasion, as Mr. Hill was standing at the door of the United States Hotel, he saw approaching him a human figure dressed in the extreme of fashion: his hat, with extraordinary ingenuity, was balanced on one side of his head, apparently prevented from falling off by the aid of a large bundle of curly hair. His upper lip was thatched. He held in his hand a little cane, with which he would occasionally beat the side of his leg, with a courage quite remarkable, considering the fragile nature of his supports. He shuffled towards Mr. Hill in the most affected manner.

"How do, Mr. Hill, deloighted to see you. I shall patronoize you, to-night, I shall, pon honor."

"I shall be happy to see you at my entertainment," replied Mr. Hill.

"Ah, much obleeged. I like to patronoize such persons as you, you are so demned entertaining: you are, pon honor."

"I feel profoundly sensible of your kind intentions of patronoizing me," said Mr. Hill, mimicing the tone and manners of the exquisite, "but I would not have you run any risks on my account."

"Whoy, it's only a half."

"Oh, ah! that is not what I meant; but I should be afraid if you should come, and be struck with an idea, it might prove fatal."

"Sir!"

"And then, sir, you know if I should chance to have the honor of waking you up to a hearty laugh, some of your gearing might give way, and no one can tell what might be the awful consequences."

"Ah! eh! you are demned funny. I shall certainly patronoize you, at all events; and I intend to bring Miss E. with me, pon honor. She is one of the most charming cree-tures you ever saw,—dresses so well, and—— ah! there she is, delightful cree-ture.—I shall bring her with me, to-night, pon honor. Bye, bye, Mr. Hill, depend on my patroinage." Saying which he departed.

If it were not for the amusing monkey antics of such fellows, it would be a fortunate thing if they could all be brained with a Webster's spelling book, or some other fatal instrument of that character. Actors are particularly liable to be insulted by promises of patronage from just such brainless animals as he who volunteered to countenance Mr. Hill. They do not look upon the actor as one belonging to a profession which requires talent, energy, and study, for its successful pursuit, but as a mere instrument of their amusement,—not having a particle of value in society beyond the emotions they can create from the stage. The actors are, themselves, in a great measure, to blame for the low appreciation put upon their art. If they were only to study the part they have to play upon the real stage of life, as they do those they represent upon the mimic one, they would not so often as now be insulted by the patronage of purse-proud asses, and ignorant dandies. But, to return to Saratoga. At dinner, on the day Mr. H. encountered the exquisite, he had the pleasure of sitting opposite the charming Miss E., whose beauties and accomplishments his "patron" had so highly eulogized. She appeared to be about nineteen years of age, rather stout, but of delicate complexion. Her hair was flaxen, her eyes blue, and her nose approaching the pug, and she lisped.

"Thelina, dear," said she, to a lady who sat next her, "have you thelected your dreth for the mathquerade thith evening?"

"Yes, I have."

"Do you know what I am going to wear?"

"Well, not precisely."

"Oh, thuch a love of a dreth. I am going to appear ath a Highland Thotch Lath. Than't I look a divinity? Mr. E. thayth he thall be perfectly enthanted, and will not allow me out of his thight the whole evening; won't that be delithous? Ma thayth—do you?—that thee really thinkth Mithter Higginth will propothe before we leave the Springth; oh, dear! eh! eh! eh!"

"Oh, scissors," said Mr. Hill, and left the table in a roar of laughter.

A FAMILY PICTURE.

MR. HILL, in one of his many visits "down east," was belated one evening, and was compelled to seek shelter at a small farm-house. He thus describes the family party and the family doings on that evening.

The heads of the family were a Mr. and Mrs. Jones, who were honored, on this occasion, with a visit from a plain sort of man, who told me, said Mr. Hill, that he teached school in winter, and hired out in haying time. What this man's name was, I do not exactly recollect. It might have been Smith, and for convenience' sake, we will call him John Smith. This Mr. Smith brought a newspaper with him, which was printed weekly, which Mr. Jones said—as it did not agree with his politics—was a very weakly consarn.

Mr. Jones was seated one side of an old pine table, and Mr. Smith on the other. Mrs. Jones sat knitting in one corner, and the children under the fire-place—some cracking nuts, others whittling sticks, &c. Mr. Jones, after perusing the paper for some time, observed to Mrs. Jones, "My dear!"

MRS. JONES. Well.

MR. JONES. It appears.

MRS. J. Well, go on.

MR. J. I say, it appears.

Mrs. J. Well, law souls, I heard it; go on.

Mr. J. I say, it appears from a paragraph ——

Mrs. J. Well, it don't appear as if you were ever going to appear.

Mr. J. I say, it appears from a paragraph in this paper ——

Mrs. J. There—there you go again. Why on airth, Jones, don't you spit it out.

Mr. J. I say, it appears from a paragraph in this paper ——

Mrs. J. Well, I declare, Jones, you are enough to tire the patience of Job. Why on airth don't you out with it.

Mr. J. Mrs. Jones, will you be quiet. If you get my dander up, I'll raise Satan round this house, and you know it, tew. Mr. Smith you must excuse me. I'm obliged to be a little peremptory to my wife, for if you wasn't here she'd lick me like all natur. Well, as I said, it appears from this paper, that Seth Slope—you know'd Seth Slope, that used to be round here?

Mrs. J. Yes; well, go on; out with it.

Mr. J. Well, you know he went out in a whalin' voyage.

Mrs. J. Yes, well.

Mr. J. Well, it appears he was settin' on the stern, when the vessel give a lee lurch, and he was knocked overboard, and hain't written to his friends since that time.

Mrs. J. La, souls! you don't say so.

Before going further, I will endeavor to give you some idea of this Seth Slope. He was what they term, down east, "a poor shote;" his principal business was picking up chips, feeding the hogs, &c., &c. I will represent him with this hat. (*Puts on hat.*)

"Mrs. Jones says I don't know nothin', and Mr. Jones

says I don't know nothin', (*laughs ;*) and everybody says I don t know nothin'; and I say I *do* know nothin', (*Laughs.*) Don't I pick up all the chips to make the fires? And don't I feed the hogs, and the ducks, and the hens? (*Laughs.*) And don't I go down to the store every morning, for a jug of rum? And don't I take a good suck myself? I don't know nothin'—ha—(*laughs.*) And don't I go to church every Sunday? and don't I go up stairs, and when the folks go to sleep, dont' I throw corn on 'em to wake 'em up? And don't I see the fellers winking at the gals, and the gals winking at the fellers? And don't I go home and tell the old folk; and when they come home, don't the old folk kick up the darndest row? (*Laughs.*) And don't I drive the hogs out of the garden, to keep 'em from rooting up the taters? And don't I git asleep there, sometimes, and don't they root *me* up. (*Laughs.*) And didn't I see a fly on Deacon Stoke's red nose, t'other day; and didn't I say, " Take care, Deacon Stokes, you'll burn his feet?" I don't know nothin', eh! (*Laughs.*)

This Mrs. Jones I have spoken of, was a very good kind of woman, and Mr. Jones was considered a very good sort of man; but was rather fond of the bottle. On one occasion, I recollect particularly, he had been to a muster, and came home so much intoxicated, that he could hardly stand, and was obliged to lean against the chimney-piece, to prevent himself from falling, and Mrs. Jones says to him, "Now, Jones, aint you ashamed of yourself? Where on airth do you think you'd go to, if you was to die in that sitiwation?"

JONES, (*Very drunk*). Well, I don't know where I should go to; but I shouldn't go far, without I could go faster tnan I do now.

As soon as Mr. Jones had finished the paragraph in the paper, Mrs. Jones threw on her shawl, and went over to her neighbors to communicate the news. I will endeavor to give you an idea of Mrs. Jones, by assuming this shawl and cap. (*Puts on shawl and cap.*)

"Well, Mrs. Smith, I suppose you ain't heard the news?"

"La, no, what on airth is it?"

"You recollect Seth Slope, that used to be about here?"

"Yes, very well."

"You know he went a whalin' voyage?"

"Yes."

"Well, it appears, from an advartisement in the papers, that he was sittin' on the starn of the vessel, when the vessel give a lee lurch, that he was knocked overboard and was drowned, and that he has not written to his friends ever since. Oh, dear! it's dreadful to think on. Poor critter!—he was such a clever, good-natured, kind soul. I recollect when he was about here, how he used to come into the house and set down, and get up and go out, and come in agin, and set down, and get up and go out. Then he'd go down to the barn, and throw down some hay to the critters, and then he'd come into the house agin, and get up and go out, and go down to the store and get a jug of rum,—and sometimes he'd take a little suck of it himself. But, la, souls! I never cared nothing about that. Good, clever critter! Then arter he'd come back with the rum, he'd set down a little while, and get up and go out, and pick up chips, and drive the hogs out of the garden; and then he'd come into the house and kick over the swill-pail, and set down, and stick his feet over the mantel-piece, and whittle all over the hearth, and spit tobacco juice all over the carpet, and make himself so *sociable.* And poor fellow! now he's gone. Oh, dear! how dreadful wet he must have got! Well, Mrs. Smith, it goes to show that we are all accountable *critters.*

A POOR SPECIMEN OF THE YANKEE CHARACTER, AND A TOLERABLE FAIR SAMPLE OF THE IRISH CHARACTER.

THE New England people are noted for their hospitality; for although they will shave you as closely as possible in a bargain, even to the paltry amount of a few cents, they do not object to give you a dinner that will cost ten times as much as the advantage they might get in a bargain. There are black sheep in every flock; and the old lady, of whose meanness I am going to relate, was one of them. A poor, way-worn traveller of an Irishman, stopped at a small farm-house in the neighborhood of Worcester, and asked for a bowl of bread and milk. This simple refreshment is usually given to all who ask the slight repast, without a wish for any other remuneration than the satisfaction to be derived from the doing of a benevolent act. The old lady to whom the poor Irishman appealed was not to be rewarded in this way, and when the poor fellow had partaken of his bread and milk, and some hard, indigestible cheese which was placed before him, he asked what there was to pay. He had but a twenty-five cent piece in the world, but he was proud for all that.

"Why," said the old lady, "seeing as how you have drank a powerful lot of milk, and our cows are very dry this summer—indeed they are the driest lot of critters you ever did see, and as for cheese, I never dew expect to see another bit of cheese as long as I live. I guess I must charge your twenty-five cents: yes, jest abeout twenty-five cents."

The poor Irishman reluctantly threw down his quarter, and walked towards the door.

"Look here, my good man," exclaimed the old woman, "you've been travelling reound a good deal, I dare say, and may be you can tell suthen that will cure the rats."

"Faith! marm, you may say that. But what's the matter wid de craythurs—what's the disase?"

"Oh! they aint got no disease. They are abeout the heartiest lot of rats you ever did see. They have gnawed clear deown from the garret into the cellar, and I do wish I could get suthen as would drive 'em away from the house."

"It's me, marm, that knows what will drive 'em away—like St. Patrick driv away the varmin from ould Ireland."

"Dew tell—there's a good man!"

"But I'll have to charge you fifty cents for it, for I'm a poor boy."

"Oh! I don't mind what I pay, if you'll only drive them away, so that they'll never come back again;" and so saying, the old lady put another down upon the one she had just received from Pat.

The Irishman put both into his pocket.

"Well, marm," said Pat, "I'll tell you what will drive them away, so that they'll never come back: you must get a large bowl—not such a one as I've been eating from, but a much larger one if you plase—fill it full of milk, but don't skim the crame off as you did for me, crumble some stale bread into it, and be sure you don't use it fresh baked, for it aint good for their little stomachs ; then let all the rats come round and ate. Don't disturb them, marm, if you plase, but let them ate as long as they've a mind to, and when they get through, charge them twenty-five cents a piece, and, by St. Patrick, they'll never trouble your house again !"

A DINNER PARTY AS WAS A DINNER PARTY.

THE announcement of the highly-successful comedy of "The Green Mountain Boy" was presented to Mr. Hill by its author, during his first appearance in Boston, at the Warren-street Theatre. The success of this piece was celebrated by a dinner, at the lodgings of its author. Besides Mr. Hill, some of those who had performed in the piece were invited, and other gentlemen, friends of the author, making in all about twenty guests. Dramatic authors are not often in a position to give entertainments, but in this case, Dr. ——, occupying an eminent position in another profession, could afford this almost incredible undertaking. The day before the dinner was to be given, the author received a note from Mr. Hill, desiring that all the company should wear white wigs upon the occasion, and also to give notice that he should take the liberty of bringing a friend whom he had accidentally met, and whom he had believed to have been dead a number of years.

In order rightly to understand the purport of all this, I must recur to some events which occurred the day before. Mr. Hill was very fond, when walking along the street, of attracting the attention of the passers-by, by making some odd quotation from the dramatic store ever at his command.

"The babe died with its mother"—"He cut her throat from ear to ear," and such like sayings. Frequently he has been stopped by some verdant news-hunter, desirous to be informed the particulars of the heroic story thus dimly shadowed forth. This was often the cue for some extravagant invention that would have made even Baron Munchausen blush.

About the time of which I am writing, there was a great religious excitement in Boston against the theatres. Fanatical ranters were denouncing everything of a dramatic character. They mixed play-acting and intemperance in such groggy proportions, that many of the well-meaning temperance advocates became so intoxicated with the doses administered, that they fell off the temperance platform, stumbling upon the stage. At this time Mr. Hill had been playing, with great eclat, Mawworm, in the Hypocrite. One morning, whilst passing down Washington-street, he was invited by a friend to drink. "No," says Hill, "I will never drink again," and seeing a seedy individual approaching—black dress, white cravat, &c.—he exclaimed aloud, à la Mawworm, "'tis true—and she cut her throat from ear to ear."

"Say, friend," said the seedy gentleman, attracted by the manner of Hill, "what did she cut her throat for?"

"Because her husband got drunk," replied Hill. "I knew her well, poor critter."

"Tell me all about it," anxiously asked the seedy gentleman.

Mr. Hill's invention never was at a loss in such a case, and he made the hair stand on end upon the head of the astonished listener, when he related the horrors which led the woman to cut her throat from ear to ear. But, however, rum is the cause of such real horrors, that little merit is due to Hill's invention in picturing forth its evils. No imagining can equal the reality.

The stranger invited Mr. Hill to his room, near by, where the tracts were printed for gratuitous distribution, by which the community of reformers hoped to chase sin from the city.

Hill told Mr. Spyman, as we will call the gentleman in black, (his real name being concealed for good reasons) that he was out of employment at present, but that he could write, and would like to compose some tracts.

Spyman thought he might do, telling him if he would write a good one against the theatres it might do much good. After discussing temperance, and other congenial topics of the day, Mr. Hill proposed that his new friend should call at No. —— Washington Street, at 6 P. M. on the following day, informing Spyman that a committee meeting was to be held for the purpose of buying up all the theatres and converting them into meeting houses, and the actors into preachers. Hill gave his name as Duzanberry. Spyman was very much pleased with the invitation, and agreed to be there, Hill also promising to meet Spyman at the tract room in the morning of the same day. Hill kept his appointment, and, as a finish to the morning's work, proposed to introduce Spyman to the celebrated Mr. Mawworm.

At 5 P. M. on the day of the dinner, there were assembled at No. —— Washington Street, twenty individuals, determined on enjoyment, and each prepared to furnish his quota of wit, song, sentiment and humor.

Mr. Hill came without his friend, but announced that he would mingle with "society" before the board was cleared. The whole party, without at all comprehending Hill's intentions, complied with his request, and appeared in white wigs. They made, as may readily be imagined, rather an outrè appearance. Two Irish lads, waiters in the house, were dressed in livery, and answered to the well-known dramatic names of Doriscourt and De Valscour. After the cloth was removed, and the wine was circulating, a general request was preferred to Mr. Hill that he should explain the object of this dining in wigs. Mr. Hill deferred his reply for the present. The bell rang, and Doriscourt came into the room, and said a Mr. Spyman was below, who inquired for Mr. Duzanberry. Mr. Hill announced that he was Mr. Duzanberry, and that the object of Spyman's visit was to have Hill read a tract. He acquainted them with his interview of the day before. The company now began to smell some fun, immediately resolved themselves into a committee of twenty, for the reception of the envoy of the Reform Club. Glasses and bottles quickly disappeared, and De Valscour was ordered to show in Mr. Spyman. Says Hill this is the text from the tract from which I shall preach :—" A house divided against itself cannot stand." All I ask of you is to keep sober, and whatever I command do it.

De Valscour entered, and following him, Mr. Spyman. Hill requested the company to rise and join with him in singing a solemn dirge, which they did very gravely.

Spyman was introduced to the company, Mr. Hill giving to each the name of some celebrated preacher. Spyman seemed a good deal puzzled with the white wigs, but the gravity impressed upon every face seemed to satisfy him of the honorable order of the meeting.

Spyman responded to the introduction, and commenced

a tirade against actors and acting, and said he had just received a note, informing him that a play actor named Hill had held forth in the theatre against reform. He then read the note, which was as follows:

"*Mr. Spyman,*

"SIR:—That notorious Yankee Hill, (a general titter in the company) is going to playact again next week in the theatre. Yours, "A FRIEND."

The reading of this note produced sundry winks and girations of fingers in the company. Hill advised Spyman to reply to the note through the papers, and commenced explaining, after the manner of Mawworm, much to the delight of his friends, and to the surprise of Mr. Spyman. At length he drew out the tract, and giving Mr. Spyman some home thrusts for his ignorance and bigotry, politely informed him that he was Mr.—— Yankee Hill, and that he could not consistently preach against actors or theatres, for you know my text, "A house divided against itself cannot stand." Spyman was astonished, and looking upon Mr. Hill with a mingled expression of sorrow and anger, lifted up his hands and departed. The company covered his confused retreat with a rollicking chorus. At his exit the bottles and glasses were brought back, and song and anecdote resumed.

The story of this committee business was soon noised abroad, and caused a great deal of amusement, for Spyman was well known all over the city. In playing Mawworm upon the stage, Mr. Hill frequently alluded to the committee, which the audience received with evident satisfaction.

THE END.

www.ingramcontent.com/pod-product-compliance
Lightning Source LLC
LaVergne TN
LVHW011214110826
845150LV00006B/1430

* 9 7 8 1 4 2 5 5 1 7 1 1 3 *